MY STORIES - GOD'S TRUTHS

MODERN-DAY PARABLES THAT POINT TO CHRIST

PHILIP BYERS

MY STORIES—GOD'S TRUTHS.
MODERN-DAY PARABLES THAT POINT TO CHRIST

Trilogy Christian Publishers A Wholly Owned Subsidary of Trinity Broadcasting Network

2442 Michelle Drive Tustin, CA 92780

Cover design by Blair Cruz

For information about special discounts for bulk purchases, please contact Trilogy Christian Publishing.

Manufactured in the United States of America

10 9 8 7 6 5 4 3 2 1

Library of Congress Cataloging-in-Publication Data is available.

ISBN: 979-8-88738-061-2

E-ISBN: 979-8-88738-062-9

TABLE OF CONTENTS

ACKNOWLEDGMENTS

Everyone starts something at some point that is meaningful to them. And in most cases, they don't do it without the motivation and encouragement of others. This is very much the case with this book. I have always loved to write but never quite understood how much I did until I felt old enough to write anything worth reading and that was meaningful enough that someone would benefit from it. Then along came Facebook, and I realized that I could actually write devotionals on my Facebook page, of course, not knowing if anyone would give them a thumbs up or not. So I started doing that.

Though as you read this book, you will realize I am an avid deer hunter, you will also find out there is nothing even remotely close to my heart as the Lord and His ways. I strive to learn His ways in every avenue of my life, whether deer hunting or, more importantly, spending time with my family or working or having fun with friends. Much of the wisdom that God gave Solomon was through what Solomon saw around him, like the ants, or simply by the interests Solomon had in his life, both good and bad. If we all pay attention to what is going on around us and not just always thinking only of ourselves, we can gain some valuable life wisdom. I am thankful for the experiences I have had and am having in life that has allowed me to learn the lessons I have and will continue to learn for the rest of my life because I will always need to grow.

First, I want to thank the Lord for all the trouble He's put me through. There's a great way to start an acknowledgment page. But think about it. Some guy sitting out on a yacht drinking ice tea and reading the newspaper isn't probably going to learn a whole lot. But take that same sailor, insert a thunderstorm coming off the shore out to meet him, and his motor and sails aren't working, and that fellow is going to learn some valuable life lessons as he fights to keep his yacht from drifting out to sea where he is going to have to be rescued. So while trials are not fun and often so painful you feel like you won't survive, I am grateful the Lord allowed me the opportunity to learn many eternal lessons through life's joys and pains. The fact that I am even an author is a complete Heavenly Father thing. To Him be all the glory!

Second, I would like to thank my children, who have been so happy for me and, through their excitement, have motivated me to push this book through. They are the joy of my life and of all of God's blessings in my life; apart from salvation, I think they are the best four blessings I could have possibly imagined. Again, thanking the Lord for His kindness to me with four incredible children.

Third, I would like to thank my brother Steve who made this entirely possible. There are a lot of things that go into writing a book, and it's not free. And it was his confidence in me that was tangible as he put his money where his encouraging mouth was and gave me this opportunity that I would have otherwise not been able to do at this point in my life. Steve, you've always been an extremely generous and kind person, and I am indebted to you for your hands-on confidence in helping me with this process... Literally!

Fourth, I would like to thank those of you who encouraged me to start a blog or write a book. To be honest, at this very moment, I have zero confidence in my ability to write anything of quality, and I have moved forward entirely on the encouragement of others, including TBN (Trinity Broadcast Network). Their acceptance of my manuscript and the kind prodding of very kind people around me has given me the courage to step out and see what might be possible.

Lastly, I would like to thank... you... the reader. We live in a very fast-paced world, and there are so many other things you could be doing. The fact that you are reading anything of mine is so humbling I can't even express the gratitude I have for you. My prayer is that the time I have taken to do everything to get to this point where you have sat down in a rocking chair or laid down in your bed right before bedtime, perhaps with a cup of tea or coffee or other drink, next to a dimly lit lamp or nightlight, perhaps late at night, that this book proves to be worthy of your valuable time. So to you, again, I say thank you! Thank you for the investment of your time. And may the lessons and truths learned that are written on these pages reach past the mental side of the brain and settle in your heart.

May the Lord richly bless you!

ADDICTIONS

Remember Fraulein Maria in *Sound of Music*, where at the beginning of the movie she is up in the mountains singing, "The hills are alive with the sound of music"? There is a stanza in that song that says, "I go to the hills when my heart is lonely." For someone like myself who grew up in the country and loved every minute of it, oftentimes, that's how I feel. Except living in a suburb of Detroit, it's mostly going to the hills in my mind, and the hills in my mind aren't quite as alive as actually being in the hills. I often reminisce about my childhood and all the incredible experiences as a dirty little country boy that I was able to have. To be quite honest with you, it's a bit of a regret that my children have not been able to experience what I did as a boy. The city just doesn't cut it when it comes to adventure unless you have aspirations of becoming a race car driver. Then you have something.

One of my fond memories of growing up as a kid in the country is the experiences of fishing that we got to have. My dad would take us a few times a year out in a small boat to catch smallmouth bass on Lake Ontario. Sometimes we would run into a school of bass, and the action would be amazing. Other times, it was as if all the fish had migrated to the Canadian side of the lake. Those were some quality times with my brothers and dad. I have to admit. My dad was much better at getting us kids on fish than I am with my kids. Having a small boat to go out on the lake helps, but I still feel like a failure as a parental charter business.

As fun as those fishing times were, those weren't my favorite. My favorite times were when we fished on the small river that ran through our little town down through the country farms in the valley, and out to Lake Ontario. We usually didn't catch lots of fish, but there was just some feeling like you were fishing where almost no one ever fished and always the expectation of the unknown. What giant beast was lurking beneath the murky, muddy waters of this river! Oh, to be able to go back and fish it now as adult with a little more knowledge of how to actually fish.

In the town, there were waterfalls that would overflow quite intensely in the fall, and after just a year or two of living there, we found out the salmon would come up the river from Lake Ontario and spawn in that little river at the bottom of the falls. And when I say salmon would run, I don't mean five or ten or twenty salmon. I mean, for about three weeks, hundreds of salmon would come to spawn. Once we realized this was happening every fall, my brother and I would spend countless hours down there running through the shallow water, trying to hook a salmon on our poles to reel in. These were big salmon, twenty to forty-plus pounds. In fact, my brother, Steve, actually caught one that we later found out very possibly could have been the New York state record at the time. We would do almost anything we could to try and catch one of these monsters. One time I even spooked one down the rapids, and the water split and ran around a small wooded island. This crazy salmon got going so fast that she literally missed the turn and swam right onto the island. That was an easy catch.

In September, we would make trips nearly every day down to the river to where the rapids ended up getting to the deep part, and we would stand there and just wait. Day after day, there would be nothing. Then around the middle of September, almost every year, we would be standing there just staring at the water as it silently, smoothly flowed toward the lake six miles away, when suddenly a fin would surface and ripple the water. Seriously, just writing about it causes my adrenaline to rise as I remember the incredible elation of what that meant for the next several weeks of our lives as we would get down there to fish as much as we could.

If you followed the falls, which were about twenty to thirty feet high from the large pool right at the bottom, it would take you straight away from the falls about 150 yards with two or three other little pools in between the rapids. Then it took a hard left where there were a couple of smaller pools in between rapids until you hit the final set of rapids that carried into the river. Those little pools were killer spots for salmon. The salmon were just feet away from you while you were trying to catch them as they bottlenecked into these small pools.

After about three weeks of pure exhilaration from fishing for these salmon, the river would go back to its old ways, silent and smooth moving toward Lake Ontario. Of course, winter would shortly set in, and that ended all the fishing altogether, as I was never into ice fishing.

I can't remember how many years we enjoyed that experience, but those were thrilling times for a young teenage boy. We rarely fished below the falls before or after the salmon run because it just didn't seem the same. But on rare occasions, we would head down there to try our skills on other fish like bullhead, pike, largemouth bass, etc. I caught all sorts of pike above the dam but rarely went below it to fish.

There was one time, though, that my brother and I and a couple of friends went fishing below the falls and located ourselves right at the end of where the rapids in the fall would smooth out into the river. We actually never caught anything that day, but something happened that literally has stuck with me and fishing that I still do to this day.

As I said, we didn't catch anything that day, but I did latch onto a very nice bass that got off, and that was it. But while we were finishing up, my brother, who had on a pretty cool pike lure, decided he was going to cast one more time. As he was casting, he said, "You never catch anything on the last cast." Like he had done one hundred times before, he reeled in his line. As he got to within about six inches of shore, we realized there was a giant Northern pike following his lure. Nowadays, he probably could have done something to entice it to bite, but as the lure got closer to shore, the pike just wouldn't commit to giving its life for the pleasure of a few skunked, scraggly, fisher boys, and it turned around and swam away.

We were going crazy at what just happened. Frustration, disbelief, and a whole host of other emotions had us throwing our lines out some more to try and catch this river monster lurking in the shallow waters.

From that day till now, whenever I am finishing up one of my fishing excursions, I always say audibly, "You never catch anything on the last cast." And you know what? I never have. You know why? Because if I did catch a fish, I would always cast again to try and catch another one. The funniest part about it is, while I would never catch anything when I would say that, it rarely was ever, *really*, my last cast. I would say it, throw out my line, reel it in and catch nothing, and say it all over again, cast out my line, reel it in, catch nothing, and say it all over again. Cast out my line, reel it in, catch nothing and say it all over again. Cast out my... I think you get the point. In trying to recreate that one experience all over again from so many years ago, to this day, I will say it, cast out my line, and repeat it multiple times until I finally don't have a choice but to quit, mainly because one of the kids has to go pee.

I've never been able to recreate that experience again, and yet, I always try, even well into my forties.

I am not sure if there is a better visual for me than to describe what addiction is like. Part of the reason I know that is because I have wrestled and do wrestle with my own addictions to this day. Mouths are falling open as you read I am admitting to an addiction. Yes, I am addicted to McDonald's cokes, medium size, light ice. I am ashamed to say in years gone by, a pop addiction would be a welcome sight compared to other ones I struggled with. And yet, most of what we learn is through failure, not success.

Those who have struggled or recognize they struggle with an addiction probably know exactly what I am talking about with this little fishing example. A lot of people have addictions and don't even realize it. But for those who do and hate it, they recognize that addiction looks something like this. They stumble, they are frustrated with themselves, ashamed, guilty, and promise that was going to be their last time, but when the shame wears off, they give in because they have to recreate the thrill of the last time again. And as a result, they live on this crazy cycle that is impossible to get off. And those who do, like one of my children having to go pee forcing me to stop, something of major catastrophe or consequence happens to them, which finally puts them in a place where they are forced to stop, or many times they finally, truly get the desire to stop.

We often don't realize when we are addicted, and yet we can be in so many different areas of our lives without knowing it. Pornography is a *huge* addiction in our society. For men, it's in the seventy percent who are regularly failing in this area. For women, it's a staggering thirty percent. Then, of course, there are drugs, alcohol, cigarettes, food, working, working out, and the list goes on and on. Some of the hardest addictions are the ones that are seemingly innocent (and quite frankly are innocent, if kept in check) like working out, working, food... Or McDonald's cokes. Did I mention medium size light ice? Just making sure. The medium size is to appease my conscience. The light ice is to get as much coke in the medium cup as possible and to help keep it cold.

Recently the thought hit me, in regards to actually drinking coke, that no bad habit will ever produce good results. But not only that, every bad habit will *always* produce bad results. So it's not like you or I will ever get away with a bad habit without suffering some sort of negative consequence. The Bible is quite clear that whatever a man sows of the flesh, he will of the flesh reap destruction. And the converse of that is, if he sows to the spirit, he will reap of the spirit, life.

For me to stop saying you never catch anything on the last cast and not cast my lure in again is not that difficult of a habit to stop... I think. But other addictions to bigger failures are much different. That is where accountability comes in. It's amazing how much having someone walk alongside you can help in any addiction, especially if they have gone through the same temptations as well and learned how to overcome it. It may take professional help in that specific area, drug rehab or alcohol programs, etc. But even if it takes that kind of intervention, it is worth it. There is nothing as liberating as learning to fly free of the fetters that previously held you captive.

Jesus' desire is to set you free. But this doesn't happen through just waving a magic wand, and suddenly your addiction is gone. He wants to teach you humility and how to fight against the urges of the flesh. Jesus said that if we are going to follow Him, we must daily take up our cross, deny ourselves and follow Him. That "deny ourselves" phrase is the hard part. But while we think we are dying, and we are, we are actually saving ourselves from a much more difficult ending than suffering the pain of daily denial. Because while it's a silly thing for me to say, "you never catch anything on the last cast," and get a little sheepish grin or chuckle from a friend, or one of my kids, most addictions left unchecked will only produce tremendous sorrow, regret, and sadly for some, even literal and spiritual death.

No one dreams of becoming an addict to anything. But if we are not careful, we can catch ourselves saying I will never do that again only to repeat that phrase hundreds of times in the future, trying to convince ourselves that after we have failed once again, we actually won't do it again, when in fact, without proper intention and help, we actually always will.

THE TRUST... PEWS?

Everyone likes a remodeling project, oftentimes so long as they don't have to do it themselves. But there are times when the need for change in a room, house... or church requires some sweat and even some blood, unfortunately, to get things looking fresh and new. Certainly, there is something of value and satisfaction in starting from scratch and building a structure from nothing. But I would say equally satisfying is taking something that is old, worn down, and even occasionally falling apart and completely remaking it while still maintaining its original form. I suppose that is why shows like "Extreme Makeover" are popular.

Anyone who does any kind of remodeling knows that before you can rebuild a project, you have to destroy it first. In the building industry, we call it "demo." We walk into an outdated kitchen with Formica countertops or a bathroom with pink ceramic tile on the walls, and the first thing we have to do is demo and tear it all out down to the original framing.

Such was the case with a recent church building project that the company I work for was doing. In fact, the church was the church I have attended for over twenty-five years. When I arrived at our church in May of 1997, the church had pews with maroon fabric, carpet that was maroon in color with lower walls that were, you guessed it, maroon.

Apparently, maroon was a smash hit in the early nineties. In total fairness, the color wasn't exactly maroon. But it was so off the wall to what is in style nowadays. I am not sure it had a name for the color. The closest color I can think of was maroon. While we have since painted the walls and added some cosmetic things to the sanctuary, the pews and carpet were still the same, that is until 2021, when we began the process of actually remodeling the entire sanctuary.

Like anything of value, you don't go into it haphazard without properly thinking the whole process through. Our church hired an architect and design firm, and they drew up some great drawings that, when finished, would propel our church from the early nineties well into the third decade of the twenty-first century.

Once the plans were drawn up and approved, the project commenced, and the church began to order material as soon as possible because of such long lead times. While we knew we were ways out with certain parts of the project, we knew if we didn't order eight months in advance, we would be waiting to install once the time arrived for us to do that particular phase of the project. Pews and carpet were two of those items we would have to order right away, which we did. And due to many unexpected setbacks, one being the passing away of a close older friend who I had worked with for twenty years and who was the brains behind the project, we were not ready when they arrived.

As every remodel project pretty much does, it took quite a bit longer than we planned because of what I had just mentioned about my friend, but also because of all the unforeseen issues we got into once we demoed walls and floors. We found all sorts of interesting things that we had no idea were there. So we had to make adjustments on the fly to make sure we did everything properly.

While we were waiting for the pews and carpet to come in, we tackled the front of the sanctuary and baptismal area first. That area alone, being the main focal point of the church, took the longest. As we were getting that mostly wrapped up with the finishing touches in the front area, I knew other phases were about to take off and managing the job. I wanted to make sure we were ready. The entire time we remodeled the sanctuary, we only missed one in-person gathering as we made sure to schedule everything during the week and then do a massive clean-up every Friday. Sometimes it carried into Saturday.

As the time approached for the old pews and carpet to be torn out and new pews and carpet installed, the pastors and I collaborated on how to best do it. This was the one time we missed in-service gathering. But we knew if we were going to install the carpet in two weeks, we had to cancel one service.

So I hatched a plan and got the pastors to buy into it that the Sunday night before carpet started that next morning, we would ask men from the church to come and help us take out the pews. There were roughly twenty-five to thirty pews that were approximately eighteen feet long. Six of those pews were in a balcony area. To be honest, I was a bit concerned about how long it would take, so I decided to come two hours early to get a head start. Before I arrived, I wasn't sure what was the most efficient way to get the pews unbolted from the floor and loose so they could be carried out to the dumpster. There was an older gentleman that arrived before me and was tinkering around with a pew, slowly unscrewing the dozens of screws in each pew. When I arrived, he had two pews loosened from the floor, and one of them he was in the process of taking apart.

That was when my twenty-one years plus of construction kicked in. There was no way his system, God bless him, was going to work in a timely fashion. Demoing and tinkering do not run in the same sentence. One of the tools you never show up to a demo party without is a sledge hammer, and thankfully, I hadn't. I grabbed my sledge hammer and started looking for the weakest points in the pews, and started hitting them. First, I hit the side piece with just a reasonable swing, and that fell off. I would then walk over to the other side and knock off the other end piece. Next, I walked behind it and would hit each leg brace, knocking it over, so by the time I got to the last leg, once I hit that, the entire pew was on the floor. The backs were still attached, but I let those stay for a bit.

In less than forty-five minutes, by myself, I had broken down every pew. By the time I was done breaking the pew down, the other gentleman was still unscrewing the backs of some that I had knocked down. He was making progress but not demo speed progress. So I took my sledge hammer, and in another ten to fifteen minutes, I had removed all the backs, and everything was in sections ready to be removed.

When everyone showed up to work, they were shocked at how far along the process already was. In fact, in just an hour, the twenty-five or so men that came had completely cleaned up the place and were ready for the carpet guys to come the next morning. While they were moving out pieces, I was ripping them in half with a circular saw. What we expected to be a two-hour process minimum only took them an hour because, in just forty-five minutes, I had, with a sledge hammer, broken all the pews into pieces.

After everyone left, I went home, got my boys, brought them back with their hoverboards, and they zipped around for a while on the wide-open floor. Eventually, that turned into a big construction garbage can in the middle of the floor, and we played basketball. As a side note, I won. The way my kids are progressing, I need to celebrate the sports victories while I am still able. Victories are going to become few and far between very quickly.

I've often thought about that pew demo project with some satisfaction at how quickly I was able to destroy those pews. But I also realized there is a great lesson, a concerning lesson, to learn from that experience.

When those church pews were installed, there was a minimum of a few days just to put them in. That was what it took for the new ones to be installed. Then for the next thirty years, those pews were faithfully used basically every single Sunday and Wednesday by hundreds of people. The amount of time spent sitting in those pews has to be well into the hundreds of thousands of hours. They had served the people well. How many conversations did friends have encouraging or challenging one another? How many times did a church leader talk and counsel one of the members, telling them not to give up, to pray, or stop living a certain way? I know from personal experience the countless hours of sitting in those pews listening to the pure preaching of the Word of God, and my heart was stirred like the men with Jesus on the road to Emaus. Many times by the end of the message, I was dying to get out of those pews so I could run to the altar and pray.

Those pews had served the congregation all those times over all those years... And in forty-five minutes, I had completely destroyed them, and the only thing left was the memory of what they had been used for.

Trust is quite similar in its function. Trust is rarely given immediately upon meeting someone or striking up a friendship, nor should it be. It is too fragile a quality. Trust is built, and it takes time. Trust is incalculable in a relationship, and as a result, it's not something that should be taken lightly or carelessly given. Oftentimes to really trust someone deeply in a way that is tangible by the evidence of what you will tell them or do for them or do with them can take years, perhaps even decades. For some, their maturity allows them to grow into it, and yet for others, they will never experience the deep trust that only comes with a deep relationship because they will not grow up and prove themselves trustworthy. While you are reading this, I am quite confident you know someone who you cannot trust. They have not made the investment into a relationship with you that will give you confidence that they can be trusted. And sadly, most of us have at times foolishly trusted someone who hadn't earned it, and we were sorely disappointed by the results of that broken trust. Broken trust, as much as anything, can make someone become cynical.

But here is the concern with trust. Like those pews that had such a long history with them and countless hours of use, deep trust is the same way and takes countless hours to build and feel confident in that trust. But again, like those pews, trust can be broken in a matter of seconds if those who are entrusted with it are not careful to protect the faith someone has put in them. You can have someone trust you for years and, in a matter of moments, break that trust. And in most cases, the trust that was destroyed can never be built back. You may get to a shell of the former bond of trust, but never to what it was. Because once it's broken, it's usually broken for good.

Sadly, to my own shame, I could point to times in my younger years where the immaturity I had didn't value the kind of trust that was being put in me, and in a matter of seconds, I destroyed that precious, fragile gift that someone had given me that was built over quite some time through relationship.

Think of David. This warrior/king is a man after God's own heart. He has made Israel into a great nation. Israel is at the peak of existence, which has taken years of ruling and wars, and in a single moment of temptation, he sleeps with one of his best friend's wives. Then to make matters worse, he kills Uriah, who was one of his mighty men. But what would have happened if David had not killed him? Do you think Uriah would have ignored and continued to trust David? Incidentally, remember Ahithophel? He was one of David's closest advisors, of whom the Bible says his counsel was like the oracles of God. He was Bathsheba's grandfather. Remember what he did? When Absolom, David's son, tried to take the kingdom from David, Ahithophel became Absalom's advisor, and he was the one who told Absalom to sleep with David's concubines. Think maybe Ahithophel never forgave David for what had happened? And certainly, there was no trust rebuilt after what David had done with his granddaughter.

Maybe you are a trusting person. Be careful who you put your trust in. The Bible actually never says to put our trust in man. That's really quite a sobering statement, but you won't find it. There are several verses. However, that tells us *not* to. Does that mean we shouldn't trust anyone? I don't think the Bible is relaying that because it does tell of the value of a trustworthy person. But the point is, be trustworthy and give your trust sparingly and carefully. As Ronald Reagan once said, "Trust, but verify." Because it can very easily be abused, leaving you deeply wounded and confused by what you thought was a pillar in someone you could lean on, only to find yourself lying flat on your face because that pillar was unexpectedly, instantly broken.

Maybe you're the person in who someone has put tremendous trust. Like Potiphar trusting Joseph, someone has told you things, or asked counsel of you regarding a very private matter, or perhaps is trusting you to do something you said you would do. Maybe they have entrusted you with an object or money to hold onto for a while, like Potiphar with his entire house. Was it earned? And regardless, do you value the trust that was given to you? Perhaps it has taken a long time to reach the level of trust you are at with someone. It's scary to think that it can so easily and quickly be destroyed and that trust be lost forever.

The thought of breaking the trust of someone who considers me trustworthy honestly scares me because I know the human heart and how prone to foolishness I am in my own heart. But in the end, I suppose that's where I want to be because fear of failing will cause me to walk carefully, protecting the trust that has been placed in me. Lest like those old worn-out pews, all the time, energy, and investment in building trust, could be torn down and destroyed in a matter of just a few foolish, careless moments of stupidity.

HOW VALUABLE IS THE KINGDOM

I believe the year was 1993. I was fifteen years old. We lived on a
country road with woods right behind our house, and directly across the
street, we had woods as well before it dropped off into a valley where a
river ran from a waterfall in a little town we used to live in out to Lake
Ontario, six miles away. As boys, my second oldest brother and I used to
salmon fish in the pools of water all through the rapids when they would
come to spawn at the waterfalls. It was really a country boy's dream.

My oldest brother was twenty-one, and he owned a Dodge Ram
50, which was basically a small size truck. It was a very cool truck, even
though it was smaller than the normal size. In the fall of 1993, the
second oldest brother and I drove it to Pennsylvania for the deer season,
which was a pretty neat little adventure, to say the least. I had already
filled my tag and was done hunting. So while my brother went hunting
in the afternoon until dark, I would take the stick shift Ram 50 and
cruise all around the dirt roads up in the mountains of Potter County,
Pennsylvania. Fifteen years old, no license, and driving a stick shift. The
four-wheel-drive worked pretty good as well, but moving on.

While this was one cool truck, it had a little problem. Basically, every
weekend, the head gasket was blown and had to be replaced. So you would
have to take off all the hoses and wires attached to the cover of the engine,
take out the spark plugs, unbolt the engine head and take it off to replace
a five-dollar gasket. Then reverse and reattach everything all over again. It
wasn't every weekend, but it felt like it, and it wasn't even my truck.

There was one particular day when my brother was yet again working
on replacing the head gasket of his little Ram 50. And as always, when
something isn't your profession, things usually go wrong. This was no
exception, although by now, I would have thought he would have been

a master at it based on his multiple gasket replacements. Among all the normal frustrations of having to replace the gasket yet again, not really being a mechanic, and quite frankly not really having the proper tools, things were about to go from bad to worse.

This particular day I was there while he was working on the engine. When I say I was there, that does not mean I was helping. It does not mean I was holding a flashlight or holding wrenches to give him when he needed one. No, I was there purely for entertainment value. You know, as every young, immature, irritating brother does just sitting there and acting like he's interested or cares, but really he's secretly mentally laughing his head off as things continue to spiral out of control at a very rapid rate of speed. And the wheels were about to fall off, figuratively speaking.

In the process of trying to put in one of the bolts, he stripped the threads to the hole. The reason was the head was an aluminum head, so the threads were not real strong, and if you didn't seat the bolt perfectly, it would completely change the thread detail, making it impossible to screw the bolt in. As a result of that little mishap, he had to retap, which simply means rethread the hole so he could put the bolt back in. While entirely possible, no one wakes up in the morning and thinks to themselves, "I sure hope today I get to retap a dozen bolt threads; otherwise, this day is going to stink." There are tools for this type of thing because he was not the first or last to strip out a threaded hole. The problem was that my father didn't have a tapping set, so my brother had to use a set from none other than his girlfriend's father. Definitely don't want to mess this one up. Certainly don't want to break it accidentally or lose one of the pieces. That would not be a good look. A lot was on the line.

He got the tapping bit that looked like the right size, which was about three inches long, half-inch in diameter, and bronze in color. Already frustrated, as you can imagine, he began to slowly turn the tapping bit and rethread the hole. Suddenly without warning, as he was turning the bit with a fair amount of pressure, you had to, the bit slipped and let loose, causing his hand to jerk from the pressure he had on it, and he rammed it into another part of the engine and tore open his knuckles. That was the straw that broke the camel's back. He lost his cool and grabbed the tapping bit and heaved it out towards the road. The road was about thirty yards away, and all you heard was one ping as it bounced off the pavement and landed in the woods filled with all sorts of nature's leftovers. He just threw a three-and-a-half-inch bronze color bit into a section of woods covered in leaves, sticks, and all sorts of weeds. Not good.

Have you ever been there? I have, recently, I think, last night. The night was late, I was trying to edit a video on my computer, and while I was editing, around seven times, my editing software crashed, losing my work and having to start over. To my shame, after the seventh time, I took my headphones, threw them on the desk, and went to bed frustrated. That's just one of many situations over the years. This was one of those times for him. Little did I know at that age what that kind of frustration would feel like as I grew up and became a big person with big problems. The problem was that this day, he had just lost his girlfriend's dad's tapping bit. In an effort to help him, I told him I would find it. He sarcastically laughed and told me he would give me ten dollars if I found it because there was no way I would. There were too many things working against me. Game on.

As he went inside to cool off from the summer heat, I went over to the road and began my search for something that appeared quite impossible to find. First, I tried to replay in my mind where I heard the bit hit the road. Was it to the left more? Or maybe the right. I never actually saw it hit; I just heard the sound when it hit the road, then the leaves. After slowly replaying the sounds and locations in my head, I began to slowly make my way off the side of the road and began looking for any possible shape that looked out of the ordinary.

I slowly separated grass blades to look in between them. I would slowly move sticks out of the way so as not to disturb the ground but rather just clear the area for better visibility. I would move leaves gently to expose what was laying underneath in case, as it bounced into the woods, it rolled under a leaf. After all, it was round, and who knows what it did after it hit the first time. Eventually, after not finding it that way, I decided to do a grid search. I knew, or at least I thought I knew, within a twenty-foot distance right to left where it would have had to go into the woods, but I didn't know how far. So I started at the road, back bent over as I carefully scanned the ground. Eyes slowly moving back and forward, taking one small step at a time.

I don't know how long or how many passes I made, but at some point, as everything looked so familiar, my eye caught something that stood out. I found it! I probably had passed over it a dozen times, but that particular time, my eyes picked it out. I proudly picked it up, took it into the house, and handed it to my brother, who had a sheepish grin on his face by now. I never did get that ten dollars, but it didn't matter to me. I had done something more valuable than ten dollars. Not only did I help my brother, but I had conquered a seemingly impossible task of finding a little tapping bit camouflaged in the woods that instantly became a treasure to me.

This story reminded me of the one in Matthew 13 in the Bible where it talks about a man who was in a field, and when he found a treasure, he buried it again, went and sold literally everything he had so he could buy that field with the treasure in it. What happened to me and my brother is not the exact same, but there are some similarities that created the same results.

I have the privilege of walking with a group of men who have chosen by their own free will to be accountable to one another in an effort to fight against the lust of the flesh through things like pornography. So many men have ruined lives because of this trap, and the men I walk with don't want to be one of those statistics. So we fight together. And the reason we fight together is that purity in this sensual, immoral world is a treasure. It is something that's more and more rare, which makes its value go up all the more. The man in Matthew 13 found a treasure to him that was so valuable he was willing to sell absolutely everything he had, just to get the field that had the treasure buried in it. Realizing that little tapping bit was not my brother's, realizing he would have to eat humble pie, realizing he would have to buy another, and the thrill of the challenge made that little bit priceless to me. And I did whatever I had to do to find it.

What do you find valuable in this life? That parable of the treasure in the field began as so many of Jesus' parables did with, "The kingdom of heaven is like." What Jesus was pointing to was that the kingdom of God was so valuable that nothing in this world is worth having over pursuing his kingdom and all that His kingdom entails.

That can be so hard in an American culture where we are given the freedom to pursue happiness. As a result, the obvious pull is to find material things, pleasures, and other carnal pursuits more valuable than God. Many of them in and of themselves are completely moral; nothing wrong with them, except perhaps how important they may become to us. How do you know if that is the case for you? What do you spend most of your time dwelling on or free time doing? Where does your mind automatically go when the pull of work lifts off your mind, or you walk away from the family dinner table, and your fatherly or motherly responsibilities are done. Certainly, the same questions apply to young adults and singles. Oftentimes with my present job, I have a decent amount of drive time. Where does my mind go in those open spaces of thinking? Is it *always* on my hobby, or... hobbies. Is it always about my personal wants or needs? Is it always about planning my next adventure? All these questions are tell-tale signs of what I find to be most valuable in my life.

The second thing that my story of that tapping bit and the story of Matthew 13 have in common is "desire." The amount of desire someone has will determine their level of success or failure. I'm not talking about me having the desire to be better than Michael Jordan, and if I have the desire, which I don't, I can do it. I am talking about things in life that are attainable for all of us. Again, going back to the accountability group I am a part of. Everyone one of the men would truthfully say they want to walk in purity. But how intense is that desire? Are they willing to go to whatever lengths they can to conquer every man's battle? For some, that may be getting rid of social media or past connections. Maybe it's getting rid of the internet entirely. No, God would *never* ask us to do something that insane... or would He? For some, it's just having accountability. It's amazing to watch a few, as I have done myself in the past, tinker around with the battle. Oh sure, I don't like it, and there is a level of disdain for impurity. And as a result, you go around the same mountain over and over again because while you don't like it, you don't have the intense desire required to conquer it. For many, this circular rollercoaster extends to their entire life. But then you see a guy, as I have had the privilege of doing, get that look. Suddenly, there is a desire that consumes them, and there is *nothing* more important than attaining their goal. And when they get there, everything changes.

The reason I found that tapping bit was simply because I was going to find it. It wasn't an option. I didn't think to myself, I hope I find it, or maybe I'll find it. For all the reasons stated earlier, it was a must-find situation, and there was no other option. I knew it was there, and I was going to find it through sheer grit and determination if necessary.

Where is your desire, and for what? Recently, I finished listening to the book of Ecclesiastes, and one thing is for sure, all of our pursuits are vain. Being the fact that they are vain doesn't mean we shouldn't enjoy them in context. But if we set our heart upon them and our desire is primarily toward those vanities, we will, like Solomon, live out our lives chasing the winds of contentment, yet never catching up to it as it will always stay just out of reach, like the styrofoam cup that blew away in the wind and every time we think we have it, a gust blows it just a little farther out of our grasp.

There is only one thing that has such value that it should consume our desires in such a way that our enjoyment of other things pales in comparison. That is pursuing the kingdom of God and the King of this kingdom. And if we have that passion, you and I will, as the Bible puts it, "Lay off every weight and sin that so easily besets us." So that we are unhindered in our pursuit of the kingdom.

The kingdom of God is there for the finding, as sure as I knew that tapping bit was there somewhere hidden in the leaves, sticks, and dirt. The question on the table is, how valuable is it to you and me, and do you have the desire to do whatever is necessary to find it?

> Again, the kingdom of heaven is like unto treasure hid in a field; the which when a man hath found, he hideth, and for **joy** thereof goeth and selleth all that he hath, and buyeth that field. Again, the kingdom of heaven is like unto a merchant man, seeking goodly pearls: Who, when he had found one pearl of great price, went and sold all that he had, and bought it.
>
> Matthew 13:44–46

KIND, HELPFUL, AND IN HELL?

Today started off like most other days. Get up, get dressed, and head to work. Once there, you start addressing all the issues or tasks that need to be taken care of, usually with your mind on the next thing on the list while trying to take care of the first one.

One of those things for me today was to get a hold of Kate, the office manager from our electrical subcontractor, and have her schedule the electricians to come out and do an estimate for us with the hope to get it going quickly. I've known Kate for around four years. Being a building company, you have to have a trustworthy electrician that isn't priced out of the market, and I wasn't happy with our long-term electrical company, so through a series of events, I found this electrical company. Her brother originally was my contact point, but when he left for other work, she quickly stepped in and took over his position.

I actually really never met Kate. The closest I came was to meet her in a Lowe's parking lot to give her a check. But I was on an important call when she pulled up, and the best I could do was hand it to her and let her know I was on an important phone call and profusely apologize later, letting her know I wasn't trying to be rude. She said no problem, and off she went, and that was the only time I'd ever seen her in person. But Kate and I have talked probably hundreds of times on the phone. Rarely do we ever do a construction project where there are no electrical jobs involved, and there were times when we would talk a dozen times a week about scheduling, bidding, and everything else involved in the process.

When it came to working with Kate from a distance, she was one of my favorite connections out of all our subs. Kate was kind. She was always respectful. She was humble and never hesitated to apologize for mistakes the electricians might have made. She was as pleasant of a person to deal with as anyone I have ever worked with in a business relationship. We rarely ever talked about anything but work, but I enjoyed calling her because, for one, I knew she would *always* pick up the phone or respond to a text almost immediately. That's huge in any working relationship, and out of all our trades, she was the only one I could count on answering when I called.

As with all of our other jobs, they were involved with the electrical at our church during the remodeling process. Again, just in the last year, regarding our church project alone, I had had dozens of conversations with Kate about the electrical at our church. We were coming down to the wire before this past Easter Sunday with where we would be with the project. We wanted to take down the curtain we had covering the front for nine months so everyone could see the progress at the front of the church. The electrical was a major part of that, and again, nearly every day for a few weeks, I was calling Kate, asking her for help to have her guys come and bail us out of one electrical issue after another. Knowing how important it was to me, she always accommodated and sent someone out immediately the next day.

Something I would *rarely* do because of my personality but felt compelled to do was invite Kate to our Easter Sunday service. She told me she doesn't go to church and that she wasn't religious at all. I made a couple of bait and switch comments, but she never took the bait. No argument, but she made it clear that wasn't going to happen. I let it go and went back into business mode.

Just a couple of days before Easter Sunday, we were again texting back and forth, and I jokingly said to her, don't forget you are invited to church, and feel free to bring your husband and seven children along with you. I knew she had been married for a relatively short time but had no idea if she had kids or not. I assumed no. She laughed at my joke and said thanks. Easter came and went, and Kate and her husband never showed. Quite frankly, I went zero of four with my Easter invites.

About a week and a half ago, I reached out to Kate again and told her that I needed someone to come and price out a job. As usual, she said no problem and gave me a list of dates to choose from this past week. I was too busy and never got back to her about the dates. But this morning, I realized I needed to get that estimate going, so I sent her a text this morning, "Hi Kate, we really need to get someone over to that job asap! Let me know what you think... " No response... Whatever... probably busy. About an hour later, I decided I'll call her because she always answers. It immediately goes to voicemail. Oh, well, sometimes that happens when they are on the other line. So I called again... and again... it immediately went to voicemail. Maybe she has the day off. The weather is nice, and she is married, so maybe she and her husband are taking the day together, good for them. I waited about an hour and decided to check a couple more times, and sure enough, both times, it went right to voicemail. I thought to myself, *Oh, well, I need to get this going, so I'll just call their office, which I have done maybe five times in four years.* I never needed to do anything other than call Kate.

I scroll through my phone, trying to find their office number to make sure I have it, and I push the send button. After a couple of rings, another lady answers the phone, "Hello," and she names their electrical company. I responded, "Hi, this is Phil from (and I named my company). I was trying to get ahold of Kate, and her phone went immediately to voicemail, so I'm assuming Kate has the day off, but I was trying to schedule you guys to come out and price a job." Silence on her end. The silence completely escaped my notice, or I had at least jumped to the wrong conclusion, so I continued. "I had talked to Kate a week or so ago, and we discussed getting someone out to look at our job. Kate is aware of it, so just wanted to see if we could schedule that. If I need to talk to Kate tomorrow, that's not a problem." That's where the lady on the other line interrupts me and says, "I'll stop you right there. We are all reeling at the moment" Immediately, my mind starts getting very worried. "Oh no, one of the guys on the crew has gotten really sick. Or maybe the owner is really sick.

I know him pretty well. That would be terrible! I hope one of them didn't get very badly injured! I like those guys!" Suddenly my mind and ears are jolted back to reality as she continues, "Kate is dead... Kate was up north this past weekend and got into a terrible car accident, and she was killed instantly!" "WHAT?... HOW?... NOO!... How is this possible?" She quietly responds, "Yea. We are all reeling pretty badly at the moment."

I am sitting there in my work truck in stunned silence while the rest of the guys are moving about doing their projects. The immediate urge is to start asking questions to understand what happened, and yet even if I were to ask at that moment as I did later in the day, it would not change the fact that Kate is dead. It doesn't matter what happened. She's dead! The ease of calling her, the pleasant sound of her voice, the very helpful attitude, the kind heart, gone, it's all gone! ... She's gone! My text to her this morning will never be answered. My missed calls will never be returned because she's dead, and death is final.

Saturday, I was recovering from a nasty cold out in the woods, laughing about a missed opportunity at a silly turkey, and Kate's husband and co-workers, and brothers were thrust into an incredible tragedy that was unexpected and incredibly sudden. Sunday, I was celebrating the marriage of my beautiful niece, and Kate's family is mourning the loss of a wife and mother, who was killed the day before mother's day. I can't imagine being her husband. She is out driving with her uncle in his sports car, and she's not coming back for too long. He begins to feel a little anxious because she's not back yet. Her phone rings but no answer, not the first time or the tenth. I've been there; I know what that feels like. I've had the anxiety come when my wife or one of my kids doesn't answer the phone. I know what that feels like. The difference is that my wife came home. My kids came home. His wife didn't. I was to learn later that she was married a year ago to her present husband, and she left behind three children from a previous marriage. Four hearts are instantaneously broken. Four lives changed forever.

Throughout the day, as I tried to keep my mind on work completely unsuccessfully, my mind remembered that just a couple of weeks ago, I had invited her to our Easter Service, where she would have heard a message of salvation. I have to be honest and say that made it worse because she said, "No thanks." As a Christian, here is what I now wrestle with, and I know of many people in the same place, Kate, who was kind, helpful, pleasant, and respectful, is probably in hell at this minute. I know, I know, the natural desire to soothe pain in this area is to say, well, we don't know what happened between my invite and her death, and I don't. But based on what experience I do have with Kate, Jesus was not the Lord of her life. You can't take all the good, fun, happy verses of the Bible and ignore the serious, challenging, and fearful ones, even at the expense of your own sorrow. The Bible said that "*many*" will go the broad way that leads to death. And hell isn't only filled with murderers or thieves. The road to hell is also paved with "good" people according to the world's standards. And yet, He was giving her an opportunity by having me step *way* out of character to invite a woman to church. That is just not me.

But certainly, the mind doesn't stop there. Could I have said more to her over the four years that would have caused her to change? Was her heart set on not serving the Lord as nice as she was, and my incessant witnessing would have upset her instead of humbled her? Could I have said something better or presented my offer in a way that would have convinced her to come?

I know everyone has their cookie-cutter answers to these questions, and they may be right. But they are not such easy answers when you have someone that was a friend who very possibly is in hell today because she very likely rejected the last offer of salvation from the Lord through an uncomfortable guy that cared enough for the relationship to try and persuade her to come and meet Jesus.

For those who aren't following Christ, you better pay attention the next time someone asks you to church, witnesses to you about Jesus, or warns you of the judgment to come. That may be the last time you are invited by Christ to become a follower of Him. And I have no doubt that some who may even be reading this are playing games with God. Oh, you're just trying to scare us into becoming Christian... Yes, I make no bones about that. I am, in fact, quite literally trying to scare the *hell* out of you. Because that is the only location for all who die apart from following Christ. And though Kate's dead, I care enough about you to be hated by you for telling the truth if you choose to reject what I am saying.

My younger brother this past November, my good friend and work partner for twenty years, Paul in January... and now Kate, a very good business friend, this past Saturday, have now all passed away. I know God is sovereign, and He does whatever He wants. He has that right, and I know He is totally justified in all of His decisions. But as long as I'm alive on this earth, I will never get used to people I love and care about dying in this world. But maybe that's the point... to hate death so much... that we pursue and continue to pursue Jesus Christ, who is the only one that provides the remedy to death by giving us eternal life if we but follow Him.

I sure hope I am wrong about Kate! Our relationship was very much primarily business-related. So it's very possible that maybe she could have met Christ, and I wasn't told. Only God knows, and I rest in His sovereignty and justice. All we can do is make sure *we* don't leave the most important decision of our lives up to chance. After all, if you are reading this, it may be the last time Jesus ever beckons you to come. Most people may go to hell for choosing to reject Christ according to the Bible, but you don't have to be one of them.

FREEDOM OVER
HANDOUTS/BONDAGE

As a boy, I was always trying to catch things. I and often my friends would set up little traps to catch critters alive so we could keep them as pets. The few times I was successful, I wasn't quite the caretaker that I realized I needed to be. If there is mouse heaven, I know about seven of them that are eating Swiss cheese and wearing halos while subordinate cats are giving them pedicures. They earned it. Strangely enough, one minute I was trying to hunt and kill animals, and the next trying to catch them for pets. I wasn't really good at catching them, which is maybe why I resorted to killing them... I'm just kidding!

Now, as a grown adult, I still feel at times that inner boy is coming out of me when I see a possible wild animal that could become a pet. To make matters worse, my youngest son feeds the inner child in me as he is a lot like his dad. Hopefully, in the hunting part as well. But he sure loves all sorts of creatures for pets. We... I mean... he... has had lizards of all sorts, some wild, some store-bought. And of course, just like his dad, he has not been the greatest of caretakers, and his little amphibian prisoners have also gone the way of all flesh.

About four or five years ago now, it was spring, and I was out scouting in the woods, probably looking for sheds, which here in Michigan, I have a better chance of winning the lottery. As I was walking between a swamp and a small lake, I was about ready to step into a shallow puddle when suddenly, right in front of me, a rather large bullfrog jumped into the water and apparently thought he had escaped danger. All it did was awaken the sleeping dirty little rug rat inside my near-middle-aged body. I really wanted that frog... for my boy! I went into stealth mode, like a tiger ready to pounce on its unsuspecting prey, and with one quick reach of the hand, I wrapped my fingers around that frog and caught him. Trust me when I say this, this was not my first rodeo when catching frogs. They are delicious! I was carrying an empty backpack due to shed hunting, and so I dropped him in, zipped it shut, and off I went. Ever heard a bullfrog growl? He was not happy. But no matter, I was.

I was so excited to get home and show my son to see the look on his face, and it did not disappoint. He was immediately added to the pet collection of a lizard and a turtle, and he instantly became the household favorite... Okay, well, me and my boy's favorite. I bought a little glass tank and put some water in it with wood chips. I would go purchase about thirty crickets and drop them in the tank and watch the frog have dinner. He never did use his tongue. He would just jump at them and catch them. Slight disappointment.

My boy had lots of fun with him. We would let him jump around the yard and even put him in a small pool. We had to let him swim around. He even nearly made it into one of my YouTube videos. There was a bond between us. In the summer, I would keep him in the garage, and in winter, I would bring him inside and keep him in the basement. Occasionally at night, that amphibious monster would start croaking, and you could hear him all through the house. I give my wife a lot of credit!

It was over two years that we had that frog, and I really wanted to see how fat that amphibian could get. Once it warmed up, I put him out in the garage on a shelf by a window that I kept open at the time. On top of the glass, I had a screen lid made for the tank that I would put over it so he didn't jump out. Most of the time, I would put a brick on top of the screen so it was weighed down. But I had gotten lazy about it over the winter, and he never tried to jump out. I trusted him. We were friends. So when I put him out in the garage, I never set the brick on the screen top because he would not want to leave me. Life for him was too good.

About two weeks after being outside, I hadn't seen him in a couple of days, so I went out to take a look, and he was gone. The lid was semi-knocked off, and he was not there. Immediately I had assumed my boy had left the lid off but upon careful interrogation... I mean... questioning; I realized he hadn't done it. For a minute, I thought maybe an animal had gotten him, but the window was five feet above the ground, and there was zero sign of any foul play, and believe me, I checked. If an animal took George, I was going to hunt it down and institute immediate and sudden capital punishment.

After doing my thorough investigation and carefully checking the yard for a few days, I had resigned myself to the fact that he was gone for good, and consequently, I told my boy we wouldn't see George anymore. He was pretty bummed. But to be honest, I think the little boy inside me was more bummed than he was. Let's just say, in my scouting the next spring, and every spring since, when I am along the swamp and lake, my eyes were looking for George's brother.

What in the world would cause a frog like George to want to escape his tank? I overfed him, He had water he could swim in and most of the time sat in. I regularly cleaned it out and made sure his environment was perfect for him. Of course, he never told me that, but I know what I would want if I were a frog. Everything seemed perfect. So why would he knock the lid of the tank and jump out the window? Freedom... He sensed the freedom in the air on the cool summer night, and he made a mad dash, or hop, for it and disappeared, never to be seen again.

The Bible says that all of creation groans for the appearance of Christ. Why is that? Because when He comes, He is going to deliver this entire world from the bondage and consequence of sin, and He is going to bring freedom to this entire universe. This world is a mess, so upside down in every way. Apart from the work of Christ in our lives, we are *all* in bondage to the thinking and ways of this world. When we come to Christ, there is a partial deliverance in the mind, but certainly not the body. That *is* coming, hopefully soon.

That frog chose freedom over all the comforts that I could give him.

For one, my perspective of what he needed was probably and most likely not accurate to what he really needed. Second, even with all the supposed comforts, his desire to be free was stronger than his contentment to be spoon-fed. Sound familiar? We live in a country where our government, or at least a large segment of the government, is trying to spoon-feed us everything. They hand out free money, give all sorts of incentives at pretty much no expense to many, open the borders and let illegal people in at no cost to them. Why? Because if they can get people to be content with someone else providing for them, then those poor souls, without even knowing it, have lost their freedom through dependency. And while many "biblical" fools may be running our government, they are not stupid, and their evil devices are intentional because their father is the devil.

But that was never God's intention for men and women to be slaves to others because of handouts. And even all of creation is yearning to be free.

Listen to our own Declaration of Independence that was carefully drafted to address this issue... "We hold these truths to be self-evident, that all men are created equal, that they are endowed by their Creator with certain unalienable Rights, that among these are Life, Liberty, and the pursuit of Happiness. That to secure these rights, Governments are instituted among Men, deriving their just powers from the consent of the governed... That whenever any Form of Government becomes destructive of these ends, it is the Right of the People to alter or to abolish it and to institute a new Government, laying its foundation on such principles and organizing its powers in such form as to them shall seem most likely to affect their Safety and Happiness."

Why did George escape? Because the world I had forced him into with all of its provisions was too small for him. He instinctively chose the uncertainty of freedom over the dependence on provision.

So the next time someone offers you something for free, whether a business, "friend," family member, government, or that old serpent, the devil himself, ask yourself, "What is this going to cost me?"

I propose to you that there are very few things in this world that are worth losing your freedom over. And I am convinced George would agree... Should have taken the frog legs when I had the chance! Seriously! They taste like chicken!

WALK IN THE LIGHT—THE EVIL ONE LURKS IN THE DARKNESS

Years ago, probably eighteen years now, my wife and I lived in an apartment in Eastpointe, MI. The apartment complex was two stories, and ours was on the West end on the first level. I actually really liked that apartment. It was a great place to start for a young couple. Nine hundred square feet, and I believe the rent was around 560 dollars a month. That's cheap, but being fairly new to the construction world and my wife being a legal alien from Guatemala, she was not able to work; things were still quite tight. Shortly after I smashed my jeep after running into my younger cousin one night on the way to soccer, I ended up with an 89 Astro van. I really liked it. My older cousin owned it previously, and he always took incredible care of his vehicles. So even though it was a 1989 minivan, it was a very nice one. Rebuilt engine, if I remember correctly.

Because we lived on the first level of the complex, the driveway was right outside our window, and by outside our window, I mean, I parked our van within three feet of our bedroom window. The driveway was much bigger, but we had our two designated spots, so I used the one closest to my window. There was a bright light in the middle of the driveway that illuminated the entire driveway for all the renters. It really worked well for us those few years we lived there.

At one point, my father, who lived less than a mile from us, asked if he could park his truck at our place for a few days. I had no problem with that, so I parked his truck in my original spot and moved my van over one space, so now his truck was between my window and my van. It just so happened that while his truck was there, the light that illuminated the driveway was out as well. That was all it took. The next morning, I woke up for work, and when I opened the door to my van, I quickly realized my steering column was all busted up. Believe it or not, I was so naïve, it took me a few minutes to finally realize someone had tried to steal my van and had failed for whatever reason. I never heard a thing that night while they tried to do it. I was able to jerry-rig a couple of wires and get it working, but the column never got fixed. Literally, one parking spot away from my bedroom window, there were thieves trying to steal my vehicle. No driveway light, and for the first time since I lived there, a vehicle parked between my bedroom window and my van. And right away, my van was nearly stolen.

The enemy does his "best" work under cover of darkness. He hates to do things under exposure to the light. One perfect example of this is found in Proverbs 7, where the adulterous woman seduces a young, foolish man. The young man had put himself in a position where he invited temptation. He walked by her house. He took the wrong path home. But what made it even worse was that he did it under cover of darkness.

Do you want to invite temptation of any kind into your life? Do it under cover of darkness... or another way to say it is... in secrecy. The enemy loves the darkness because if he can keep someone in the darkness, in secrecy, it's like separating a young calf from the herd of cows, and it's pretty much easy to take the calf down from that time on. He has the upper hand, and you, as long as you stay in that darkness, are doomed to repeated failure.

In all my years of fighting temptation myself and walking with others who fight temptation, I have never won the battle by keeping it to myself, living in secrecy, or staying in the darkness. And believe me, because of pride, I've tried. It has only and *always* been when I stepped out of the darkness into the light of accountability that suddenly I gained the upper hand on temptation, and it felt like the chains that held me captive were suddenly breaking.

The enemy wants you in darkness because there, he can lie to you and get away with it. He wants you to believe you are the only one, and if you are honest and open, you will lose credibility and respect with others. Most importantly, in the darkness, he can condemn you and keep you separated from your Heavenly Father.

Tip #1 from Proverbs 7 is to *stay away from "her corner."* Don't willingly put yourself in a position to be tempted. Tip #2—*turn on the light.* Bring the temptation to the light through accountability, and the temptation will lose its upper hand, and you will find strength to fight... And quite frankly, not have to fight alone.

Maybe the temptation has gone too far, and you are giving in to it in whatever area of your life you are being tempted. It's especially important for you to humble yourself and bring it to the light because as long as you keep it hidden in secrecy, you will be a prisoner of that failure. The best-case scenario is to bring it to the light in the conception stage of the temptation. As the famous saying goes, "Nip it in the bud."

Because here is the thing, both the young foolish man and the adulterous woman thought no one noticed. But there was a man in the window looking down on them. So it is with God. There is no darkness, and nothing is hidden from His sight. What you think you are keeping secret, the Bible says, will be shouted from the house tops. Then what good will your secret be then?

Why not bring it to the light now and address those temptations or failures in the clarity of the bright light? Not all temptation is avoidable. But all temptation is subject to the light if we are willing to humble ourselves and turn on the light switch.

I have a challenge for anyone who fights temptation of any kind and has the guts/humility to try this little tip. We live in a world where there are multiple ways to connect to people. Here is my challenge next time you are tempted with anything. Men, to look at pornography perhaps, or maybe buy that gun you can't afford. Or maybe it's even to say something you will regret. Ladies, to look at pornography (believe it or not, that needs to be said these days), to buy that thing you know your family can't afford but you really want, to gossip or slander that person because they have hurt you... The moment you feel that temptation coming on that No one knows but only you, take your phone, pull up your contacts, and find your very closest friend that you can be brutally honest with, and they will support you even in failure and send them a text simply saying, I am feeling tempted right now, and I just wanted to bring it to the light, so it's not a secret anymore. I double-dare you... And watch what happens. Watch what happens when you turn on the light switch to your struggle.

What would have happened if the man watching from the window had had a spotlight to shine down on those two foolish people? The adulterous woman would have immediately covered her face and ran away, so hopefully, no one would have noticed it was her and what she was doing. And the foolish young man would have likewise run away because he wouldn't want to have gotten caught either.

Next time you're tempted, just do that. Turn on the spotlight to the secret temptation, and suddenly that temptation will flee from you like a roach when the light switch turns on. A simple text could literally change your life, if you will but do it... How do I know? Been there, done that... And it works... if you have the courage to do it.

Why does it work? It's as simple as can be and right there in front of our faces in the Bible... "God resists the proud... but gives *grace* to the humble." It is really that simple. Any expression of humility we manifest automatically releases the grace of God, His divine power, into your life to accomplish what you need to accomplish. And a simple text is often all it will take to release God's grace. You don't believe me? Muster up the courage to try it just once and watch the temptation flee away like a scared coward.

AVOIDING TEMPTATION

Temptation is such an unrelenting thing. Certainly, it rears its ugly head in different ways, but it's odious nonetheless. I'm not sure due to our sinful nature; it will ever completely go away, lessen maybe, but go away completely, I don't think so. The best you can do is manage it. Of course, it comes in all shapes and sizes for different people, and each situation can have somewhat of uniqueness to it simply because everyone's lives are different. What triggers one person may not trigger another though both situations are a mirror image. And yet, that other person gets triggered by their own devices. And then, of course, certain things that trigger people do not trigger others... men are more tempted by lust for the opposite sex than women. Women, I dare say, struggle with covetousness for material things more than men... generally speaking, of course. Food can tempt one person and not another or certain kinds of foods. I'm not the healthiest eater by any stretch, and fast food and pop are definitely a temptation. I could eat a sausage McMuffin and drink a medium coke... light ice from McD's... every morning if I could afford it. It just hits the spot. I know I'm not alone. And often, the same temptation can drive people into much more serious situations. But as I've already stated, temptation, while persistent, can be managed if we are intentional.

Proverbs 7 is a rather uncomfortable chapter because it talks about a man being seduced by a harlot... and he gives in. It goes into quite a bit of detail on how she seduces him, and he, like a lamb, is led to the slaughter, the whole time thinking he is going to gain some pleasurable experience, which for the moment he may until the bill is due for his recklessness. But due to the detailed description of his folly, there are some incredible lessons to learn on how to manage and even avoid, to an extent, temptation.

The most obvious one to me is found in Proverbs 7:8. He was going down the street near her corner, walking along in the direction of her house. His first and probably biggest mistake was that he put himself in that position. He was near her corner, walking toward her house. What in the world was he doing? Just asking to be tempted.

So many times, we willingly, usually because we unintentionally put ourselves in temptation's way. We are told to pray "lead *from* temptation and *deliver* us from the evil one," and yet we then walk down the street near "her" corner, metaphorically speaking.

I was reminded of that today as it was roughly 9:30 a.m... I hadn't eaten breakfast, and I was headed to an appointment... and wouldn't you know it, it was... right... past... a well-known stop I had made many times. At McDonald's... on the corner... hmm, sound familiar? I am happy to say amidst the temptation to satisfy my drooling taste buds, I drove on by. But that temptation was entirely my fault. I put myself there. I knew where it was, and yet I allowed myself to go that route, knowing I would be driving by. My brain had already planned the whole event out 4 miles ahead of time. And, of course, it was the "fastest route." So there was a good reason. Here's the thing, it was the fastest route... and sometimes temptation is unavoidable... but why did I have to drive in the lane closest to their driveway? Why didn't I get in the fast lane farthest from a simple blinker and turn? Why? Because I was flirting with danger! I was toying with temptation. I passed the test, but not with flying colors, as they say.

The problem is we often put ourselves in temptation's way where the stakes are much higher than some extra calories and eventual cholesterol issues. Some things are life-changing for us, including those around us. But we put ourselves there the whole time, hoping nothing happens.

The best way to manage temptation is to avoid it altogether. It's to be intentional about staying away from "that corner" to begin with. Because while that corner may be a shortcut. It may not be the shortcut you expected, and you and I could find ourselves very quickly in a place we were not intending.

ARE YOU LAWLESS?

Matthew 7:21, "Not everyone who says to Me, 'Lord, Lord,' shall enter the kingdom of heaven, but he who does the will of My Father in heaven. Many will say to Me in that day, 'Lord, Lord, have we not prophesied in Your name, cast out demons in Your name, and done many wonders in Your name?' And then I will declare to them, 'I never knew you; depart from Me, you who practice lawlessness!'"

Do you realize that pretty much the only group who claim to prophesy, cast out demons, and do wonders in Jesus' name are Charismatics, Assemblies of God, Pentecostals, etc.? I certainly don't see that activity from Baptists, Presbyterians, Lutherans, etc.

My point isn't to diminish any denomination or promote one over the other. They are all man-made. But my intention is to point out that doing or claiming to do great things in Jesus' name is not the criteria for getting into heaven. He didn't confirm or deny what they did or didn't do. It was irrelevant to their entering into God's kingdom. There was only one thing that disqualified them. They were lawless. These people had feigned Christianity and great spirituality in front of people and possibly doing great miracles, but when it came to their personal lives, they disregarded the law of God, and they were thrown into hell.

Of course, the question could easily be asked, were they saved by works? The obvious answer is no, and yes... well, not exactly yes, but if you don't think works matter, then you don't understand what salvation really is. James made it quite plain. James 2:18: "show me your faith without works, and I will show you my faith *by* my works." No, works do not save you, but you and I best better have some works in our lives to show that we have genuine faith.

Jesus made it about as plainly as one could make it. "*If* you love me...

Keep my commandments." True salvation by faith causes a person to live to find out what God says about things and follow them only by the grace of God.

I have told my children that there really is only one way that they can really show me they love me. It's not giving me gifts. Many people will give gifts to deceive, manipulate and get something in return. It's not saying nice things. Even the devil deceived Eve into thinking he had her best interest in mind with his words. No, there are very few, and maybe there is only one true way for me to know they love me. Live within the boundaries of my home and seek to obey my commandments. The key motivation is the word "love." Love only comes through relationship, and relationship breeds love, love breeds desire, and the cycle continues to spiral into higher levels as the relationship continues in sweet communion.

A true Christian is a follower of Christ. What are we following? We are following His example. What was His example? Well, His example had to do with a cross and death (Matthew 16:24). Then Jesus said to His disciples, "Whoever wants to be my disciple (follower of Christ) must deny themselves and take up their cross and follow me." What are we denying ourselves? Pretty much everything in the world *isn't* denying themselves.

Whether it's Facebook or many other avenues of connecting with those who profess Christianity, I see so many giving in to the pull of the world on their lives, the sound of their words, the way they look, the way they dress, their complete attention on themselves whether it's beauty or success, their conversation, and all their time being wrapped up in worldly pleasures and wicked entertainment, even taking the Lord's name in vain. Are they Christians? God will be the final judge of that, and I certainly want to fight criticism from an attitude of pride as all those same desires are pursuing me every day. That is what I am trying to deny myself. But the criteria to know if someone is going to heaven isn't really that difficult for the one who is genuinely concerned about their eternity.

Are you truly a Christian? Well, I read the Bible! Yes, but are you lawless? I go to Bible studies! But are you lawless? I regularly attend church. But are you lawless? I sing in the choir! Yes, but are you lawless? I teach Sunday school every Sunday! But are you lawless? I preach on Sundays every once in a while! Yes, but do you obey the law of God? I am the pastor of a good size church! But are you lawless?

I have a nationally known ministry!! Amazing, are you lawless?

I have an international ministry that supports lots of missionaries!! That's wonderful, but are you lawless? I gave an incredible prophecy that came true!! So did Balaam. Are you lawless? I cast out twenty demons at a revival meeting in Jesus' name!! YES... BUT ARE YOU LAWLESS??

The unsaid wonderful truth about this passage is that everyone is graded on the same criteria. Whether a king or a pauper, God will judge you based on your obedience to Him. Because your obedience to His ways and commandments are the fruit that will show whether your salvation by faith was genuine, or fool's gold.

James 2:18:
But someone will say, "You have faith; I have deeds." Show me your faith without deeds, and I will show you my faith **by** my deeds.

James 2:19:
You believe that there is one God. Good! Even the demons believe that—and shudder.

Today we remember a barren cross and a vacant tomb to celebrate a risen Savior! But don't call yourself a follower of Jesus if you, or I, are not willing to surrender to His Lordship.

It is not enough to come and hear the word of God. We must come, we must hear, and we **must** obey. Through all of life's failures, which are too many to count, if that is our heart's desire and life's goal, we are going to hear a much different phrase from Jesus. "Well done, good and *"faithful"* servant! Enter into the joy of the Lord"!

Second Corinthians 6:14–17:

Be ye not unequally yoked together with unbelievers: for what fellowship hath righteousness with unrighteousness? and what communion hath light with darkness? And what concord hath Christ with Belial? or what part hath he that believeth with an infidel? And what agreement hath the temple of God with idols? for ye are the temple of the living God; as God hath said, I will dwell in them, and walk in them; and I will be their God, and they shall be my people. **Wherefore, come out from among them, and be ye separate, saith the Lord, and touch not the unclean thing; and I will receive you, And will be a Father unto you, and ye shall be my sons and daughters, saith the Lord Almighty.**

WORKS MATTER!

HIS TRIALS ARE MOST IMPORTANTLY TO REFINE YOU

You know how many times I've heard someone say to me that the Lord is using my trials in my life to use me in a special way? Most likely, if you have shared your trials with anyone at some point and time, who is a Christian, you might have heard that. It sounds nice and certainly is meant well by it. The idea that God is refining us so that He can use us brings comfort to our hearts and gives us the strength to continue to face life's challenges.

But is that necessarily true? It may not be. Not everyone is called to be a Billy Graham, Chuck Swindoll, MacArthur, or Piper. Maybe the reason God is putting you through a trial and refining you is simply for you. Maybe there are no big plans to use you or me in a significant way in life. Maybe the lessons of our pain will not reach very far. No book, no sermon, no interview with *Focus On The Family*.

Think about it for a minute. Is there any better reason for God to refine you than He is just simply concerned about you and making sure you enter eternity in the best possible position you can? Why can't God simply just put you and me through the fire to refine us... simply... for us? He can. And while the idea of doing something great for God and His kingdom is a wonderful desire and idea, God is not obligated to use any of us in that regard. The way I see it is, the fact that He may have no big mission for me in life to affect the world, and yet he continues to work on my life in such detail and relentless pursuit expresses in a deeper way His intentional love for me personally and makes me more grateful to Him realizing there isn't some other intention for why He may be doing what He is doing except He loves me.

Your refining may not be for the world. It may be almost exclusively for you. But that should cause your heart to leap with gratitude because, in a world of over seven billion people, He notices you and has taken you and me on as His personal projects. And we know that His promise is that He will complete what He starts. Anything else He may choose to do through us, however big or small, is simply an added benefit, and the whipped cream on top (I hate cherries) to being on the Potter's wheel and letting Him fashion us how He chooses.

GOD'S WAYS ARE NOT OUR WAYS

Can you imagine being Gideon? He's supposed to deliver Israel from the Midianites and Amalekites, and it says they were like locusts in abundance and camels too many to number. The poor guy starts off with 30,000 men, and in one comment of asking whoever is scared to go home, in just half a verse of reading, he's down 20,000 men, with only 10,000 left. Sixty-six percent of his tiny group was gone in a single comment. Next, God tells him to pick out the ones He chooses, which were the ones who lapped water, and that ends up being a whopping 300 men, which is zero point one percent of the amount he had when he started! We know why God did it. He didn't want Israel to glory in themselves. See, they were used to winning battles where they were outnumbered... But not by ninety-nine point nine percent outnumbered.

Think of poor Gideon, though, as he's walking around picking the ones God chose on average; he walked by thirty-three people before he got a guy who was lapping water. What do you think was going through Gideon's mind as this was happening? Probably the exact same thing that would go through your mind and my mind. We often forget these Bible characters where people like us. They felt sorrow, joy, pain, temptation, and fear, just like we do. The Bible says of Elijah that he was a man with passions just like us. One of the things that has really been a benefit to me in appreciating the stories of the Bible is inserting myself in their shoes. What would I have been thinking as my "rag-tag army" got dwindled down by ninety-nine point nine percent? Needing lots of confirmations like Gideon would almost for sure have been needed, and God obliged. I used to be so critical of Israel after they came out of Egypt... but what would my response have been when I walked for three days without food or water for my little ones, my wife, and myself. I'm fighting frustration over a backed-up sewer that a plumber will have fixed in an hour! It's easy to criticize until I have walked a mile in their shoes.

One of the best ways to learn and appreciate the stories in the Bible is to imagine yourself in that position. I know for me, it has helped temper my critiques of those in the Bible that "weren't so awesome" and better learn the lessons that are meant to be learned... with humility.

In Gideon's case, the Lord really had a sense of humor... although at the time. I'm sure Gideon would have been of a different persuasion... as I'm sure I would have as well.

Bible stories aside. What about our criticism of other people we know, but we really don't know everything? We make critiques based on twenty percent information, thinking we know the whole story. Oftentimes I find out, sometimes years later, that I was so wrong and had no idea what I was talking about. Their situation was much more complicated than I realized, and had I known what they knew. I would have responded the same way.

I have had to counsel people who were in almost exactly the same shoes as I was, and it was so easy to tell them what they should do. But when it came to my own situation, I had such a hard time doing what I told someone else to do. It's really easy to jump to conclusions. But the faster we do, generally, the better chance we are wrong.

Part of the lessons of the stories of the Bible is to realize that these were real people with real issues that faced real struggles, including times of doubt and weakness. It's to help us understand that, for one, we are not alone with our struggles and failures or lack of faith. But also to remind us that we shouldn't be so quick to jump to critical conclusions. Because you never know when God may decide to put you through the wringer and expect something of you that is greater than your ability. He always will teach us. At that point, may we learn the lesson when it comes to others, not to jump to our own critical conclusions so quickly. We will have found out it's not as easy as we thought.

GRAFTED IN COMES WITH ALL GOD'S BLESSINGS

I was recently reading through Joshua, and I was reminded of a story that is often skimmed over, not realizing that there are some incredible truths that can encourage those of us who are followers of Christ... and a warning for those who aren't.

The two parts of the story are found in Joshua chapters 9 and 10. Israel comes into the promised land. They put a royal beat down on Jericho, and after taking care of Achan and family for the sin they committed, they set up a battle plan for Ai and ended up destroying that entire city and everyone that was in it. Unlike Jericho, they were allowed to take the spoils of that city, which they did.

Israel was riding pretty high, and their fame had reached the neighboring cities. Things were not looking good for the people living in that land. In fact, God had told Joshua to kill everyone in the boundaries of the land, He was going to give Israel. Take no prisoners. For those of you who think God's greatest attribute is love, I would beg to differ. Truly God is love, which we will see even in this little devotional, but He is first Holy, and His love is expressed in perfect balance through His holiness. But that's a rabbit trail I have no intention of going down. God tells Joshua to destroy everyone in the promised land they come into contact with, and Joshua, who was an amazing warrior, intended on keeping that command of God to perfection.

Well, a nation called Gibeon saw what Israel had done to two nations already, and they knew their goose was cooked. So they hatched a plan. They feigned distant foreigners who came from a "very far" country and wanted to make peace with Israel. You see, God did not give Israel the entire world. He gave them a piece of land in the middle east that they could inhabit and claim as their own. If you were outside that boundary line, you could be friends. If not, well, things weren't going to go well for you. Gibeon was inside the boundary line, and as a result, they were supposed to be destroyed with the rest of the nations.

Some of the Gibeonites, dressed in ragged clothes and used worn-out water bottles, made themselves look like they had traveled a long way. When they came to Israel, they had told the leaders they had come a long way and that they wanted to make peace with Israel. Long story short, not only did Israel not ask the right questions and investigate enough, they did not ask God about it, and as a result, they made a covenant of peace with the Gibeonites. A whole lot of comments and comparatives could be made about those two things when it comes to not investigating and not asking God, but that's yet another rabbit trail I don't want to go down.

Israel finds out just a couple of days later that the Gibeonites are their neighbors, but they can't do anything to them because they made a vow or covenant with them. This part cracks me up when the Bible says that Joshua asked them why they had lied to them. Seriously Joshua? Was it really that hard to figure out? You just slaughtered two countries, killing every single person aside from Rahab and family, and you wonder why the Gibeonites might have hatched a plan to save their skin? I'm not a detective, but I think the evidence isn't that hard to find and is quite overwhelming in this investigation.

When all the dust settled, Israel decided to make the Gibeonites their servants, and they were to be "hewers of wood and drawers of water for the congregation and for the altar of the Lord." I'll come back to that in a bit.

So from being sentenced to death by God via the Israelites to just a few days later, being connected to God's people and made to serve.

Here is where the story gets incredible to me and has an amazing truth that can be so easily missed. In the very next chapter, chapter 10, the surrounding kings hear about what Gibeon did, and they weren't happy and decided to band together and destroy the Gibeonites. They are in deep trouble now. First, they were going to be taken out by Israel. They make a connection with Israel, and now they are going to be destroyed by the neighboring nations... except... they had just made a league with Israel. So, Gibeon knows it's about to be attacked by these other nations, and what do they do? They reach out to Israel and say we need help. Come help "your servants."

Here is Israel's chance to get rid of their mistake. They shouldn't have made a league with them, so now let someone else take them out, and then you get out of your word without it being your fault. Pretty logical if you ask me. Except that's not what happened. The moment Israel swore to make peace with Gibeon, what was at Israel's disposal was now the Gibeonites as well. It tells us in Joshua 10 that Joshua assembled *all* the men of war, the mighty men of valor, and they went out to fight and defend the Gibeonites. But not only did Israel keep their promise because Israel was now attached to Gibeon—God honored Gibeon and fought for Israel that day, so much so that somehow He kept night from falling until Israel had completely defeated the kings that went out against Gibeon. The Bible says there was not a day like it before or since. God's commitment to Gibeon was because of the covenant Israel had made with them.

What is amazing about that story is that God was going to destroy the nation of Gibeon at one point, but because Israel made a foolish mistake and allowed them to be part of their nation, God honored that commitment and fought for Gibeon as if there was no difference between them and Israel... because there wasn't. Read 2 Samuel 21 about what happened to King Saul's family after he died because he made a breach with the Gibeonites. It was just one more example of how serious God's covenant to Gibeon was.

God has always had a people of faith that were His. He decided in His foreknowledge that the way to salvation was by faith in Christ alone. Before the cross, it was for those who believed in the Messiah to come, and after the cross, it was those who believed the Messiah came. Just because you were part of Israel did not necessarily mean you were a person of faith. There were a lot of wicked people in the nation of Israel that God destroyed because of their wickedness. But those who lived by faith in the coming Messiah, like Abraham, Moses, Joshua, Rahab, Ruth, and the list goes on, were part of God's Elect or chosen people based on their faith in a coming Messiah.

We see this in the New Testament, with the Gentiles being "grafted" into the seed of Abraham. Those gentiles who lived by faith in the Messiah were grafted in, according to the book of Romans.

Here is the incredible truth, as plainly as I can put it. We, just like Gibeon, were on the outside of God's people of faith. Because of our sin, we deserved death and destruction just as much as the natural Gibeonites were going to face certain death. But, just like Gibeon, once we became part of the people of God, every promise of God's blessing, every promise of God's protection, and every promise that God promised His people from literally before time began is now *our* promise to hold on to and reap, to the literal point that we along with all of the people of faith in Jesus Christ will become heirs "WITH HIM" of the world. Why? Because we spiritually, like Gibeon naturally, became attached to the people of God. From death one moment to eternal life and privileges the next, simply through surrender to the Lordship of Christ.

That truth alone is quite an energizing truth when we grasp the reality and eternality of that statement. But here is the second truth I want to point out. It says they became hewers of wood and drawers of water for the congregation (the people of God) and for the altar, again, from being sentenced to death to becoming servants of God's people and of God Himself by preparing the wood to make altars of worship for the Lord. The moment we become part of God's people, we are called to serve the Lord and serve each other, thus fulfilling the two greatest Commandments in scripture, loving the Lord and loving people. And really, there is no better position to be in.

The biggest takeaway from all this is two-fold. If you are a Christian

(Christ-follower), being part of the people of God comes with incredible benefits on earth and eternally. Every promise He has made to His people includes you and me. And the promises only get better on the other side of this fleeting life. For those of you that don't follow Christ and haven't surrendered to His Lordship, you don't seek to live by and obey His Commandments. You are under the judgment and curse of God, just like every nation in the promised land that would not surrender to Israel. None of the benefits are yours. None of the promises are yours to hold on to. Romans 8:28 does not apply to you. All things do not work together for your good because you are no child of His. The great chapter 3 of John that says Christ loved the world so much that He gave His life also says that every day you reject His Lordship, you are "abiding under His wrath." And all the judgments He has for the wicked will be yours one day to endure for eternity.

The wonderful thing is, like Gibeon, it doesn't have to be that way. You can surrender to Christ's rule and be guaranteed to inherit all the blessings of all the people of faith before you. The daily benefits He gives His children will be yours to enjoy... If you will only believe and surrender.

The story of Gibeon is a short two-chapter story in the Bible that can be read through in a matter of minutes. But if we really look into what the point of the story is, it can change our perspective and therefore change our life. The Gibeonites made the smart choice (albeit through deceit). Hopefully, if you haven't yet, you will while you still can. If you have, all of God's promises are yours. And He *never* breaks His promise.

TRUST GOD

I see a lot of people getting pretty anxious about what is happening in our world today. Non-stop social media posts about one thing after another that is falling apart in our society, and it is falling apart in front of our eyes. I certainly get it. I know I catch myself at times starting to get a little worked up, thinking and saying things like, "It doesn't have to be this way" or "It's not just." Certainly, our ever-crumbling world is going to have a pretty big impact on people's lives, and not good either. Definitely not for us "common folk." Wicked politicians create one crisis after another, and here we are, stuck in the middle of it. We all are and will be affected by it. But today, in my Bible reading, I was reminded of something. Just a little perspective changer as I drove by many super high-priced gas stations trying to maintain peace of mind.

Mark Chapter 8: Jesus has been teaching people for a very long time. In fact, three straight days and they had nothing to eat. Only Jesus is a good enough speaker to keep people's attention for three days when they are hungry. In this particular passage, Jesus feeds 4,000 people (many believe that was just counting the men, not women or children) with only seven loaves of bread to go around. If that's not amazing enough, there were seven baskets of bread left over. He didn't supply just enough. Leftovers, one more proof that mothers are doing the work of the Lord.

This wasn't the first time He had done this. He already had fed 5,000 people (again, believed to be just counting men) with only five loaves and two fish. So with a combined two fish and twelve loaves, Jesus fed at a minimum 9,000 people... with a combined nineteen baskets of food left over.

I was once again reminded that as a follower of Christ. Our president is not my provider. Politicians are not my provider. Other countries' oil is not my provider, and quite frankly, my place of employment is not even my provider. My job is the present avenue of my provision, but not my provider. Jesus is my provider, and He doesn't need any of these earthly avenues to provide for our needs. Oh, we might have to curb our entertainment practices. He never promised that. But He did promise through King David by the inspiration of the Holy Spirit, in Psalm 37:25, that He would never abandon his people or see the righteous begging for bread. Praying for bread, sure, begging, not so much.

Even in these perilous times, those of us who are Christians should not be in turmoil about what is going on. Certainly, we have a human element to our emotions, and all of us at one point probably feel a little anxiety about what is going on in our world. But once you get into God's Word, as I was fortunate enough to do today, because I need to every day for an eternal perspective on this natural life, you will see that we have nothing to fear. Jesus is the only one that can create something from literally nothing, and He comes through with His greatest provision when we are in our greatest need.

As Isaiah 12:2 says,

"Surely God is my salvation; I will trust and not be afraid. The LORD, the LORD himself, is my strength and my defense; he has become my salvation."

Not only can we trust Him for salvation, we can trust Him for provision regardless of bleak circumstances.

GOD'S BLESSING IN HARDSHIPS

Food for thought... Just because life is hard doesn't mean that the blessing of God is not on you. Joseph was sold by his own brothers, in a place he didn't want to be, obeying orders by a person he didn't know, taking care of a house that was not his own, being pursued by a woman he didn't want anything to do with. I know how I think. If any one of those things were to happen to me, I would be wondering what in the world I did wrong, and yet, the blessing of God was on Joseph's life. The blessing of God is not determined by social status, economic status, job status, physical health status, or popularity status. But rather, it's determined by surrendering to the leading of the Lord and going along with His program, trusting Him in the valleys. When you can trust Him in the middle of the trial, that is where you will find His blessing, even if it's being the slave of a pagan jail keeper in a faraway country.

COMMUNICATE

Last night, I spent a little bit of time watching my oldest boy play a game on X-box called *Rocket League* with a friend that lives about forty minutes away. They were playing other teams from around the world, I guess, and they were doing pretty well. They were winning, but about three games into it, I told him it was getting late, and we had church in the morning. He asked me if they could play until they lost, and considering the bracket or level they were playing in, I assumed it would be pretty quick, so I agreed and sat down to watch. They wore headphones and talked on the phone, and bantered back and forth the entire game to work together as a team. Some of the banter is quite funny as they heckle each other over their mistakes. But their communication was quite effective in playing against the other teams. They seldom were bunched up together fighting for the same ball, and often, they were making great passes to each other to give each one a great opportunity to score. And of course, I was there on the sidelines, coaching them along the way... and heckling as well. It's intentional. I'm trying to teach him to perform under pressure for future school basketball games. At least that's what I tell him.

What I expected to be a few games tops turned into five because they kept winning. Oh, by the way, Rocket League is where you drive vehicles and hit the ball and try to get it into the opposing team's goal. Basically, soccer with cars. Pretty soon, it was six and then seven, and they just wouldn't lose. Eventually, it was past 1 a.m., and I was completely caught up in their games. Slapping high-fives when they scored and... um... getting upset when they got scored on. There are reasons why I don't play these games!

They kept playing and kept winning and everything from their communication to hitting the ball at the right time just kept propelling them to victory. It was really quite entertaining to watch. After a while, my boy's friend told him that his phone was at two percent and that it was going to die any minute. Sure enough, right at the end of the twelfth game in a row that they won, his phone died. Now they had to play without being able to communicate. Immediately I thought to myself, *this should be interesting*. And it was.

Both of them are pretty good players and had worked together well the entire night. But now, they couldn't talk the way they had, and right from the get-go, the game was completely different. They were bumping into each other and going after the same ball. They weren't in the right place when the other one deflected the ball off the wall to set up a shot by the teammate. They had managed to keep the game tied because of some clunky lucky plays, but it had me at the edge of my seat because it just felt like it wasn't going to end well. It didn't.

They managed to make it to overtime, where the first goal wins. About a minute into it, the opposing team, from close range, hit the ball toward the goal. Both my boy and his friend went for the ball at the same time. Unfortunately, my boy's friend hit his car and knocked him out of the way as the ball went into the net, and they lost. We were all pretty dejected as we went off to bed at nearly 2 a.m. They had lost the game, but I had seen a very valuable lesson that I made sure to tell my boys around the dinner table the following night.

The lesson is simply this. As long as they were communicating, they were winning every game. In some of the games, it seemed for sure they would lose because they were down, and yet they worked their way back and would win in overtime, all the while talking back and forth and working together. In the very first game, where they couldn't communicate, they lost. Coincidence? I think not.

That scenario holds true for every single relationship you and I are in. The only way to have a good relationship or to be successful in that relationship is through communication. The moment communication is hampered in any way, that relationship starts to deteriorate. Unfortunately, that is often a process that can take years, especially with married couples. They get so busy living, working, and taking care of a family that they stop communicating, I mean really communicating. As a result, they start to drift apart. A husband and a wife can get so busy working that they just don't have time to talk. They become two ships passing in the night, as the old saying goes. Oftentimes a mother gets consumed with raising kids, and she doesn't stop to talk with her husband. Let's face it, though, in most relationships, women are the stronger communicators, and if they stop talking, the husband sometimes doesn't notice and doesn't try to make up the difference. I can go all day without talking to a single person and feel like I had a productive day. When it comes to communication, I certainly have to work harder at it than my wife and even a couple of my kids. But lack of communication is not healthy, and I would dare say it is probably one of the biggest, if not the biggest, reasons marriages fall apart.

But it doesn't happen only in marriages. It matters in every relationship, including with our children, especially children. It happens in the workplace. It happens between friends. Life happens. People get busy, and the relationship starts the spiral downward. It doesn't mean you will ever become enemies. But to have a deep relationship, you will have to have consistent communication! Sometimes good communication means fighting. If a relationship between two people never involves fighting, there is a really good chance that relationship is not a healthy one. One is either so dominant that the other is afraid to say anything, or the other just complies with everything because they don't want to fight it out. I'm talking about a healthy fight. But even in fighting, there is communication, and if two people are teammates, they will come to an agreeable decision for both if they are on the same team fighting for the same goals.

Communication involves intentionality. Some have to be willing to listen as much as talk. The Bible says we are to be quick to hear and slow to speak. I am fairly slow to speak, but am I quick to hear/listen? Moving on... While we may have a God-given need for communication, actually doing it regularly often doesn't come naturally. The other night I was so tired, but my daughter wanted to talk. It wasn't anything important but just talking. It was pushing 2 a.m. before I went to take a shower and go to bed. Why didn't I just tell her I had to go to bed? Because I want to have a great relationship with my daughter. I want her to know she can talk to me anytime, and I will always be there to listen. Because I know that the moment I turn off the listening ear, the communication stops, and from there, the relationship begins to deteriorate. But that takes work. And I certainly am not perfect, but it was one night I got it right at the expense of sleep.

Communication is not easy, but it's a must for any healthy relationship, whether wife, children, friends, or most importantly, with God. As I was reminded once again watching my boy and his friend take on the world of Rocket League, you cannot be effective with a lack of communication. Incidentally, tonight as I was writing this, he and his friend won a tournament for the first time ever. Surprise, surprise!

PAY ATTENTION TO THE MAN
BEHIND THE SCENES

I think I'm a decent pet owner, a bit devious at times, but a decent one! I have these two Brittanys that we got from a fine couple down in Virginia. That's an insane story in itself. We went down to get a dog, and we came home with a dog and a friendship that I thank the Lord for to this day. That was nearly seven years ago now! I can't believe how time flies. Well, two years ago now, we decided to get another Brittany, and there was only one person we would even consider buying from. My friend in Virginia. One of his females had a litter, and he let me know he had some available. The price was right, as in free (super kind of him, especially for what he could get monetarily for the quality of Brittany's he breeds), so even though we were in lockdown due to tyrannical orders by our governor, John Hopkins has come out recently and said they were a complete waste of time, me and my two daughters, under the cover of "essential" driving, made the trip down to Virginia to pick up another dog. A puppy in quarantine is essential. I believe it is around a nine-hour trip, so we left early in the morning, drove to Virginia, picked up our dog (nearly ended up with two), spent some time fellowshipping with our good friends, and then drove home through the night. It was a whirlwind of a trip but an awesome experience to share with my daughters, aside from the one getting car sick and throwing up a few times on the way down. Dramamine saved the trip home.

That was two years ago, and now that little puppy isn't a puppy anymore. But she still acts like one. If there is a dog that has ADD, the younger one has it. The seven-year-old is becoming like a granny that unless she is hunting for squirrels in the backyard, she would rather sleep than do anything else. The young one is like the Tasmanian devil... but with a good heart. She can't help it! If you let her outside after a night of sleep, she literally doesn't know what to do with herself. Turn away for five minutes, and she will dig a hole in the yard the size of a missile crater. The upside is I don't have to cut her front nails as a result. The downside is that she has cost a *lot* of worms their homes. Senseless violence, if you ask me! Eventually, she calms down and comes back to sanity after our yard looks like Swiss cheese from all the holes. Of course, every hole has a stick, bone, or a toy in it because she has a "no hole left behind" policy.

This little one just demands attention! She will not be denied. Just ask my one daughter, who is literally, as I am writing this, cleaning up from a potty-trained dog that just peed on her bed because she was ignoring her. I take back the good heart comment. It's black as pitch! But the older dog, due to jealousy, has become even closer to me and often looks for attention from me. I think she just wants to know she is still #1, and she is. Oftentimes she will walk up beside me when I am busy doing something and just sit down next to me, waiting for me to notice her and give her some love. Occasionally she will even get a little playful and try to get me to play with her by wrestling or playing with one of their stuffed squirrels. I often do for a bit, but eventually, I'm ready to move on, and sometimes she is not. This is where the devious owner comes in. I will get playing with her for a little bit and get her growling and play biting at me when I get her on her back, little legs kicking everywhere as she wiggles around trying to get my hand as I poke her body. Well, the little one gets jealous and can't stay away, so she will come over and want me to mess around with her. But I'm smarter than her... sometimes. As she is about to climb or jump on me, I push her onto the old fat one, and immediately, they start going after each other. After a second or two, to make sure their attention is now on each other, I get up and walk away, and all you can hear in the other room is those two rascals going at it, playing tug of war with a stuffed animal or just simply wrestling trying to bite each other. Mission accomplished, attention redirected as I slip away in silence. I always laugh about it because it was so easy. Works every time!

As funny as that scenario is, there is one much more devious than myself, whose name is satan, and that is a very popular tactic of his when it comes to destroying relationships. How often have you been enjoying the company of a wife, husband, friend, brother, sister, or fellow employee, and somehow, within seconds, something changed, and you are now fighting or arguing with one another? Couples who go to church are especially aware of this. You are getting ready for church, which requires nothing more than getting dressed, fixing yourself up a little bit like you do every single day, and heading off to church. But amazingly, fights so often break out as you are in the process of getting ready or on your way to church... to worship the Lord. The irony! And the entire service, all you can think about is how mad you are. Suddenly, the preacher says amen and snaps you back into reality, and pretty much the entire benefit of church that day was missed. Been there, done that.

My dogs have no idea that I set them up and then walked away. They each want to play with me, and next thing you know, I'm gone, and they are playing/fighting with each other. Sometimes I will hear a yelp or a growl that sounds different, and I know that playtime is over. satan is so clever in injecting thoughts into our minds, and we can speak out what we think, and suddenly we are in a heated discussion. All the while, he has slipped away as if he never was involved. Or maybe we say something, but we just "happened" to touch a wrong nerve with the other person. He never really slipped away. We just fail to recognize his influence in our lives as if he was never there, to begin with. But the Bible says that satan has one agenda, to steal, kill and destroy. The Bible says in Ephesians 6:12, "For we wrestle not against flesh and blood, but against principalities, against powers, against the rulers of the darkness of this world, against spiritual wickedness in high places." You say, "That person who is yelling at me looks an awful lot like flesh and blood to me," when in reality, that person is often just the vessel that satan craftily coerced into starting a fight. Have you ever been in an argument over the stupidest thing? There is a good possibility you were hoodwinked into a fight where you didn't even realize satan had metaphorically tossed you onto the other dog, and you often will look back and wonder what in the world happened? I would venture to say that in "most" instances where two people are fighting, there are spiritual forces in the background and if both parties would stop for a second and recognize what is going on, they could unify and come to a much easier conclusion than having to give apologies... four days later.

Maybe you're in a bad relationship. Maybe it would be wise to consider who you are really fighting against. Remember, in most relationships, the other party is really on your team and does want to work things out. Not always, but generally speaking. The problem is the enemy has caused all sorts of trouble in your relationship and has been completely ignored and not called to task on it. He is the master at slipping back into the shadows after he has created the fight. Incidentally, when I refer to satan, I am not referring to him specifically but rather the principalities and powers and rulers of darkness that serve him. Satan is not omnipresent like the Almighty God is.

I often tell young men and women when I am discussing purity before marriage. They will often point out a young couple that seems to be so happy living in immorality outside of marriage, and I tell them, "Of course, the enemy has them right where he wants them, living outside of God's ways." Why would he fight them? But the moment a couple gets married, often, suddenly, things seem to begin to fall apart, or at least they start to fight over things that they had never fought over before. This recently happened with a young man and woman I was counseling with. Naturally, because marriage is the closest, most pure example of Christ's (Bridegroom) relationship with the church (Bride), satan hates millions of mini examples roaming the earth always as a reminder of what Christ's ultimate intention and victory will be. Unfortunately, so many married couples completely miss the unseen agitator. But he's there. If someone walked into the room where those dogs are wrestling, they would have no idea that I started it because I'm gone, not visible, and left no evidence behind. And yet, it was entirely my doing.

There is a balance because we are fallen sinners, and our fleshly desires and self-centeredness get us into plenty of trouble without any help from our demonic enemies. But you can be sure that when a fight breaks out, the enemy is there to pour fuel on an already burning fire. He knows what nerve to touch. But sometimes, he will even light the match. If we can realize this, we will spend more time uniting to fight the same enemy than fighting amongst ourselves while our enemy gets away unscathed. Pay attention. Usually, it's more than two that are involved in your disagreements. And the one you can see is probably not your biggest problem.

FANNING THE FLAME

I had a young man who I greatly respect privately wish me a happy birthday this one particular time. And in his message, he thanked me for inspiring him and others to stay on the straight and narrow. It was humbling to think that my life could inspire anyone. But it made me think back in my own life on how men and women who I thought were so old were inspiring me to stay on the straight and narrow. Certainly, when I was a young boy into my teens, my dad and my mom certainly inspired me. I saw their faith as genuine, and it made me want to follow in their footsteps. To this day, I have implemented many, many truths I have learned through their parenting and pastoral leadership as I grew up. I remember seeing my mom worshiping on the piano until, at thirteen, I began to play my saxophone in front of her during worship time, but all the musicians followed the lead of the piano. The piano would follow the worship leader, and the instruments would follow the piano. To this day, I *love* to worship. Whether I am leading, playing my trumpet, or singing, I am in my element. I feel I am right where I belong. There is pretty much nothing in life that is more enjoyable and precious to me than being at church worshiping with other people. My mom passed that torch onto me and the brothers mostly by example. Her desire spilled over into my life, and to this day, that desire hasn't been quenched.

Likewise, my dad, as the pastor, would stand in front of the congregation and preach Christ and the cross Sunday after Sunday. His zeal for truth and his desire to see others walk out a holy life went past my little ears and landed in my heart. In a sense, my father's God became my God. I don't know when it happened exactly, but it did. Oh, I know when I got saved. I could take you to the room in the back of the house and show you where the couch was up against the wall. I could show you where I got the spanking from my mom and then where she kindly led me to the Lord. I was five years old. I will never forget that. But even after that, at some point in my young life, I really made the decision out of clearer understanding, perhaps subconsciously, that I was really going to serve the Lord. Like they say in a marriage, "forsaking all others so long as you both shall live." With my growing understanding of what it meant to be truly saved, I had decided that I was going to forsake the pursuit of this world and follow Christ wherever he led me so long as I lived. Much of that desire came from the fire I saw in my dad. My dad was an excellent preacher! He, like most all his brothers, was gifted in preaching. He had a way of pulling you in. He could tell the story at the right time. Say the right funny thing and then almost immediately pierce your soul with conviction from the Word of God. I miss his preaching. He was a master!

The weird part about all of this is that, when I remember much of his preaching where he seemed very old, he was actually the age I am now, mid-forties. He seemed so old, and that age seemed so far away. Except, this is where I find myself now, which brings me back to that statement about me inspiring others to walk the straight and narrow. When I read that young man's kind words, I had to ask myself, how bright is my torch right now? And, how bright will it be when it comes time for me to pass my torch on to my kids or the next generation? Will I allow age to fizzle out the flame, or will I make my limited time be the wind that blows on the flame to make it stronger and brighter?

You see, we all pass on something. We can't help it. Our actions and attitudes will have an effect on those around us. Especially your children, if you have them. If you are a worldly person and love the things of this world, your children will not walk away from that unscathed by your actions. You will pass something of detriment on to them. They may overcome it, but your actions have thrown them into a battle of denial that will take everything they have and the grace of God to let go of the pleasures of this world. But the same holds true if you live an upright life and your torch burns bright for the kingdom of God. Your children, your friends, and your coworkers will be affected by it. They will not be able to escape the glow of your torch, and it will only have a positive effect on their lives. Whether they choose to embrace it or reject it, it will be their choice. But they won't be able to deny its reality.

What about you? How is the flame of your torch? Do those who look upon your torch see a flame or smoldering embers? I remember as a kid watching a few times as a person would run for some time with the torch for the Olympics. I don't know how far each one ran, but after a while, they would pass it on to the next person. By the time it got to the last person who would then light the cauldron, the torch was still as bright as the first person who ran with it.

As grateful as I was by that young man saying I inspired him, his text inspired me to continue to shine brighter, to fan the flame even more. So that when that day comes where it's time for me to pass my torch on to my children, and others that I love... and perhaps a few more the Lord has entrusted to me, the light of my torch with make their eyes squint and their faces glow from the heat and the brightness of its unquenchable flame. And they will have no other option but to run with it lest, by their apathy, the passion of my flame consumes them! Retirement may be a legitimate natural thing, but it never should be a spiritual thing.

Time is short. Fan the flame!

LOW HANGING FRUIT GETS LOW LIFE ATTENTION

Ladies, especially young ones, whoever you may be, this one is primarily for you. But I think the guys will be amused as well.

I did something *insane* once. I'm still not even sure what I was doing, but I had this feeling and just went with it. Anyone who *really* knows me knows this was so out of character for me that they would be completely shocked... Want to know what I did? I still can barely believe I did it. It was a tight rope, and there was a part of me that was even concerned about doing it, but I had to give it a try. Here it goes. I can't even believe I actually went through with it.

I privately messaged a young lady on Instagram who I had no idea who she was. Nope, it wasn't business. It was to gather intel about her and maybe if she stuck around long enough to help her. As I am even writing, I'm getting goosebumps just thinking what in the world I was doing. But I couldn't help it. My Christian instinct and somewhat of a fatherly instinct kicked in, and I just went with it. So, here's what happened.

I have an Instagram page where I will occasionally post things on there to bring attention to my small business or YouTube channel. As everyone knows, you get people that like your pictures, and oftentimes, you will get people that will follow your page. When someone follows me, I will often check out their page as if it's something of interest to me, and I may follow back. You get a lot of people that will try to follow you, but their posts are nothing but trouble, and I will block them. Usually, in the form of a woman who thinks because she flaunts God's gift of beauty, I am going to want to follow her. Happens on Facebook as well. What they don't realize is that I pretty much do not friend the opposite sex. There are few exceptions and always will be. Quite frankly, I don't go looking for

Facebook friends. They come to me, and I decide based on their profile if I want to be friends with them or not. Probably not a great business strategy, but that's just how I do it.

I had made an Instagram post, and this lady followed me and liked a bunch of my posts. Nothing looked suspicious about her profile picture, just a picture of her face, so I clicked on it and saw her profile and saw some of her posts that she had made, which were mostly pictures of herself. I will get back to that. But then I read her little bio, and it read something to the effect of, "single, never been married, never had kids, a good Christian lady." I guess from just life experience I could tell there was a whole lot packed into that one sentence. I stared at it for a few seconds, and something inside me felt like I had to message her. You will know why shortly.

So, I sent her a private message and told her I would like to have a conversation with her if she was willing. I told her there was no hidden motive, but I just was hoping to ask her some questions if she would be willing to answer. That night she responded. My honest opinion was that she thought maybe I would be a possible connection for her which I quickly, carefully, and gently dispelled that notion. I told her I had been married for over nineteen years and had four kids. If she had seen a pic of me, I think she would have realized very quickly it had nothing to do with a relationship. But amazingly, she agreed. Just by her profile, when it came to her relationships with the opposite sex, I knew whatever it or they had been, it had not been good, which she later confirmed.

So, after a few more suspicious (rightfully so) questions on her part, she allowed me to ask her my questions.

Backtracking just a bit, I did ask her if her guy had to be a Christian, and she said no. I graciously showed her that if she is a Christian, the Bible is very clear on the fact that she should not marry a nonbeliever. I mentioned to her that based on her standard, maybe God had protected her from having a relationship with the wrong person because she did not hold to that standard. I gave her a few examples of why that would not be a good idea. At that point, she told me, "True. I can't deny this conversation." Not sure what that all meant, but she was clearly intrigued. I couldn't believe she was going along with it. So then I asked her this question, "If you could pick five things you would want in a guy, what would they be? And, if you could pick five things you would want a guy to see in you, what would they be? This is where it got interesting! It took a few minutes, but suddenly, I got a comment back. She had listed five really good things that, as a man, I would want to be for my wife. And the five things she listed about what she wants her man to see in her, I would want to see in my wife. They were *all* really good answers. Here was the interesting part, not a single one of the things she mentioned was about how the guy looked or about how she hoped he saw her in her physical appearance. That was interesting enough, but here was the most interesting part, all of her pictures that she posted of herself would have suggested to any guy that one of the main, if not the main, characteristics she would want a guy to see about her was her physical appearance. Her pictures weren't terrible, but every single one of them was done in a way that would draw attention from any man to certain parts of her body if he didn't make a careful choice to focus on her face.

This young lady was discouraged from looking for a man and had past bad relationships. She wanted a man with excellent character, like I said, the kind of man I strive to be in my own life, and yet she was trying to get that kind of man with low-hanging fruit... easy attraction. And then, clearly, from our conversation, she had not been happy with the results.

Deer, specifically a buck's body, will get longer as it matures. A one-and-a-half-year-old buck will not be as long or stocky as a mature four-and-a-half or five-and-a-half-year-old buck. As a result, when it comes up to an apple tree, any buck can grab the apples off the ground, and certainly, apples will attract all sorts of bucks. But the young bucks can only stand up so high to reach the apples still in the tree. The more mature bucks that are longer can stand up higher and get the apples out of the reach of the more immature bucks. The little bucks have to wait until the apples fall. So, in essence, the higher apples are the better apples because they have not been chewed on by the other deer. Other than a stray worm here or there, most of those apples are untouched.

If you're a lady or a young lady reading this, you may be wondering, "Is he calling my gift of physical beauty low-hanging fruit?" Yes, yes, I am. Let me let you in on a little secret. When it comes to physical attributes, you win. Due to God's divine creative intention, if there is one thing you *don't* have to worry about attracting a man with, it is your physical attributes. It is just the way we are wired. Even the world knows this, which is why we are bombarded with sensual images all the time. Every man is immediately always attracted to the physical beauty of a woman. It's just the way we were created. Blame God... And Eve. Adam would have never eaten that fruit if Eve hadn't started it. *No, I'm not bitter!* You exploiting the beauty that God gave you is only going to attract the immature young bucks that all they care about is beauty. I believe most, if not all, normal women would find that repulsive if that was all a man cared about, and they should. And yet, so often, that is what a woman is trying to use to attract the man to her. Like I said, you can get the young bucks for sure! But the more mature bucks, which are still attracted to beauty but care more about the purity on the inside, will walk by and get to the high apples that the other ones can't get to.

Do you know what was sad about that conversation with that girl? As a mid-forty-year-old man that has learned a fair amount about this topic, for various reasons, I offered to maybe give her a slightly different perspective than what I know she had. She was not rude at all, literally not in the slightest, but she mentioned that she believed God would bring the right person along at the right time and never allowed me to mention to her that perhaps she was looking for the right guy, the wrong way. I didn't force my opinion on her; I gave her the opportunity to let me know if she wanted it or not. It didn't appear she wanted it, so we kindly ended the conversation. I told her I would pray that she finds the right man (which I have). And suggested being involved in a church is the best place to start. She told me that she enjoyed the discussion, and we ended it, and I deleted our messages and moved on. As I said, that was extremely out of character for me and will continue to be so. But I learned a lot through that little discussion.

What I just told you about low-hanging fruit, I would have told her. I am fully convinced that most women want a genuine man whose primary reason for loving her is not because of her body. And yet, I see a lot of women out there walking around as if the only way they are trying to attract a man is with their body. By the way, that is in the church just as much as outside the church. You ladies have *so* much more to offer than the gift of beauty. As I said, I guarantee you that is not something you have to be concerned about! I'm not saying neglect it, but you don't need to flaunt it. The kind of man you want is looking past the beauty of what is inside. Beauty is fleeting! And eventually, all that is left is what is in the heart.

So just a thought to the ladies. If you are looking for a man and not having any success, maybe you're using the wrong method to find the right person. Maybe God has been merciful to you to not allow you to find the guy yet because He is protecting you from the kind of guy that you *really* don't want, and yet, those are the ones you are attracting. It's something to think about. If you already have a man, then your gift of beauty is his alone and not supposed to be shared with anyone else, intentionally or unintentionally.

I know this is a crazy topic. But motivated by having two beautiful teenage daughters, I want them to use the right method to attract the right men. I share this experience in the hopes that any single woman who may read this will protect her outward beauty by flaunting her inward beauty, thus attracting the mature bucks while ignoring the foolish self-centered bucks that only care about low-hanging fruit.

VICTORY NEVER COMES EASY... WHY?

Have you ever wondered why there are things in your life that you can't seem to get a handle on, maybe a sin of the flesh, a bad habit, or an addiction? Bad habits can start pretty young and last an entire life if we do not do what is necessary to conquer them. Oftentimes we pray and ask the Lord to make it go away, only to find out it appears our prayers are not answered.

Years ago, there was a particular sin in my life that was driving me nuts. I would say it was an addiction in its own right, and as bad as I wanted to get over this sin, I just couldn't seem to get a handle on it. One Sunday, our church held a service for the church leaders to pray for those who needed God to move in their lives, and I went up for prayer and asked to be prayed over for this weakness. I wanted it gone forever. The Pastor and his son graciously prayed over me, and I felt so energized. I was ready to take on the world, and surely, I wouldn't struggle with this sin anymore. After all, I had prayed to God, so He was going to answer me, right? Well, three weeks went by, and suddenly, I slipped back into the same old pattern I had before. Why? How come God didn't deliver me like I asked. You will sometimes hear of people with an addiction of some sort, they get prayed over, and they are immediately delivered. I've heard of a bunch of scenarios like that over the years. But most of the time, that is not the case. To walk out of most addictions takes serious hard work. And believe it or not, in most cases, that is the way it's supposed to be. Why?

Recently I was working with a young man regarding something in his life he had opened up to me about, and he has been extremely determined to fight it and not let this weakness control his life. I have had the honor of walking with him through this journey, and the other day, he asked me the same question. Why? This is what I have learned in my own life experience with what I mentioned earlier about my own struggles.

If you will remember, there were two reasons why God did not destroy the inhabitants of Canaan for the children of Israel all at once. The first is in Exodus 23:29, where the Lord tells Moses he will not drive all the Canaanites out at once because if they did, then the land would be filled with wild beasts too numerous for the people to handle. These weren't coyotes or wolves. No, just lions and bears, nothing too serious. The point is that like the all-wise God knew of the Israelites, in our own lives, if we take care of one thing in our life, we often don't fill it with something else, and so that void ends up being filled by another weakness or addiction and oftentimes worse than the one before.

I had a friend who, before I knew him, was an alcoholic. He got involved in AA, and he told me that they had all these guys beating their alcohol addiction, and at break time, they would all go out and smoke a cigarette. They took care of the alcohol problem, but they filled in the void with another addiction. In some ways more unhealthy than alcohol. Jesus mentions this in Luke 11:24:

> When the unclean spirit is gone out of a man, he walketh through dry places, seeking rest; and finding none, he saith, I will return unto my house whence I came out. And when he cometh, he findeth it swept and garnished. Then goeth he, and taketh to him seven other spirits more wicked than himself; and they enter in, and dwell there: and the last state of that man is worse than the first.

The issue was the guy cleaned the house, but he never filled it with something else, and as a result, his latter situation was worse than the first. God knew this, and so He didn't want wild beasts wreaking havoc on the children of Israel, so He slowly gave them victory so they couldn't conquer one thing and be overrun by the next. God knows your weaknesses, and one of the reasons He *may* not allow you to get complete control of your weakness is because He knows you won't fill that void with something of value. So, He's actually protecting you from being in a worse situation than you may be fighting now.

The second reason, which was more of my situation and I think most people's situation, for those that care anyway and are trying to fight the sinful nature they have and not allow their flesh to control them, is in Judges 3:1 and 2. "Now these are the nations which the LORD left, to prove Israel by them, even as many of Israel as had not known all the wars of Canaan; 2. Only that the generations of the children of Israel might know, to teach them war, at the least such as before knew nothing thereof." There was a whole generation that came up after the Israelites conquered much of Canaan land and had mostly rest that knew nothing about what it was like to fight and be in wars. It was for those inexperienced warriors that God left enemies in the land to teach them how to fight.

The purpose often in our lives is to teach us to be warriors. I know that was what I was supposed to learn through my own journey. Quite frankly, I had to learn not to be a pansy, to take the struggle seriously, and learn how to fight back. To not just go down the same trails as in times past but learn to take the high road and all the internal fighting that came with that. And if my journey of learning to fight is now helping to teach a young man or young men what it means to fight against their own weaknesses, it was worth it. Because while deliverance is nice, it doesn't build character. Character comes from getting knocked down and getting back up again... hundreds of times. Character comes from learning your internal enemy and learning how to live on the high ground, so you have the advantage when it rears its ugly head. And then, of course, character comes by humbly passing along to others what you have learned through many trials.

One of the reasons your weaknesses remain is to protect you and teach you to fill the void with things of value as opposed to leaving the cleaned area in your life empty. Ultimately it will be filled by something. The second reason is to teach you and me to fight and to be warriors.

The Christian life is not for sissies. It is standing against the very natural desires that we all have and saying *no*, I am going to deny myself these temporary pleasures for something of higher value, something eternal. And that's not easy. Especially in a culture that says chase your dreams, you deserve to be happy. If you want it, get it. Act on feelings. But if you are going to learn to deny yourself these things, you will have to become a warrior and learn to fight.

My point to all this is simply this. The very thing in your life that is driving you crazy is actually a blessing. It's building something of quality in you that you would have never had for your benefit or the benefit of others if the Lord didn't allow you to learn through failure.

So, don't get discouraged. Don't try to run from the fight. Don't complain that you still are fighting. Embrace it. Pick up your sword and shield, and like David did with Goliath, it says he "ran to meet him." And if you fall, get back up. People are much more critical than God! Every time you get up, He will be right there to continue to help you. Because what you see as a temporary frustration, He sees as an eternal blessing.

WE CAN TEAR DOWN OUR HOUSE WITH OUR OWN HANDS

Something to think about... Remember how when Moses and Aaron brought the first two plagues by the hand of God, and Pharaoh's magicians were able to do the same thing? Do you realize that Pharaoh was making the same things that God was using to judge and destroy their nation? Pharaoh's heart was so hardened. He was literally helping God destroy his own nation that he was over by recreating the same plaques God was putting on them.

The first time which wasn't a plague, Moses throws down a snake, and the magicians mimic it. While that's not necessarily destroying the nation, I have a hard time believing that everyone was thinking the more snakes, the merrier. The actual first plaque was turning the Nile river into blood. The Bible says they couldn't drink the water as a result. So what does Pharaoh do? He has his magicians replicate what God did, making matters worse for his own people. The second plague was the frogs. The Bible says that frogs come up and virtually get into everything, even their ovens. So what does Pharaoh do? He has his magicians create frogs, which help destroy property and irritate the Egyptian people. They added to the problem instead of alleviating it. The Bible says that the land stank. Invariably, those dead frogs were some that Pharaoh's magicians had created. After the second plague, the magicians were no longer able to mimic what God did, so much so that they admitted it was the finger of God.

My point to this is that when someone's heart is hardened, they will self-destroy (if that's even a word) the very desires they have or things they want. Oftentimes that reveals itself in marriage. The husband wants certain things from his wife, but his heart is so hardened to her needs that he destroys the very things he wants (often sex) by his stubborn actions.

For the wife, she often has expectations of her husband that he may not be meeting at the moment, and instead of supporting him regardless, she fights or tries to control thus taking away any desire he might have to meet her needs in the way she is hoping for. She destroys the possibility of getting what she wants/needs due to her own actions that create the exact opposite results of what she is looking for.

This scenario of self-destruction plays out in all sorts of various relationships. The 1st response is to look at ourselves and evaluate if maybe there is hardness in our hearts that is causing us to miss out on the very things we may want. Because the hardness of heart drives our actions, and actions reap results, always negative, I might add.

The second scenario is to evaluate the relationships you are in, and maybe it will help explain "why" a certain person is acting the way they are. You want to bless but can't because boundaries continue to be crossed in a way that you cannot accept. Maybe it's because their heart is hard toward you. At a minimum, it will help you pray for their hearts to be softened as you ask the Lord to continue to keep your heart softened. Maybe it will help you adjust your tactics relationally to help them soften their heart. And just to quickly add to that. Giving them what they want is rarely the answer. At least not in the way or by the method they want it.

In my short life of, well, over forty years, I have seen this scenario play out many, many times where someone is literally helping to destroy the very thing they are hoping for. It's really sad. If Pharaoh's heart wasn't so hard, you could have told him that he was helping to destroy his own nation by creating what God used to judge them, and he would have stopped immediately. But his heart was so hard. He was assisting God in doing the very thing he was upset that God was doing through Moses and Aaron and didn't even realize it. Some of the most blind people on this earth are those with hardened hearts.

Just a little food for thought when it comes to our relationships, first with God, second with those around us.

MAKE THE BEST CHOICE YOU CAN

Life is full of adjustments, and oftentimes, decisions have to be made on the fly with no time to really contemplate your choice. You make the best decision you can at the time, and it's only after the results of the choice that we can look back and contemplate whether it was the right one or not.

This was the position I found myself in over this particular weekend during Ohio's deer season. I had planned to hunt during the late muzzleloader season and spent a couple of trips going down to southern Ohio to prepare for the upcoming hunt. There was a particular buck I was after, and for the last week, nearly every day, he was walking in front of my camera during daylight hours. I felt my chances were pretty good.

In the meantime of my preparation, my wife and I made another quick decision on the fly (pun intended), and she flew to Guatemala and was away for the weekend. With some middle-aged teenagers, I didn't feel like I needed to cancel my trip, but as a father, at least for me, the desire to be their protector still made me a little cautious. I know it's going to be really hard when they jump from the nest and learn to fly on their own.

I left at 9:30 p.m. Friday night. I got about fifteen minutes away from my spot at 2:45 a.m. and parked in an abandoned parking lot to get a few hours of sleep. At 5:45 a.m., the alarm went off though I am not sure I really needed it since I slept so poorly in the truck. When is an automotive company going to come out with a work truck that actually can lay down the seats and make a reasonably comfortable bed? Anyway, I got dressed in zero-degree weather, I might add, and drove to my spot.

I made it to the blind pretty easily and got set up and ready for the hunt. To be honest, I don't remember a hunt I've had where I saw so many deer. The zero-degree temps had them moving. The sunrise was remarkable! Other than getting up so early, mornings are my favorite time to hunt. I love watching the sunrise on a clear, crisp morning.

Not long after, it was daylight. An eight-point buck I had probably dozens of pictures of showed up. If that other buck was not around, I would have not even hesitated to take this buck. It wasn't real big, but big enough for me to end my season on. He, with several other smaller bucks, fed for quite some time. Let me tell you when it comes to eating. Deer don't like to share. And if you're one of the smaller bucks, oh well, you will have to wait your turn. After some time, the bucks left the field, and I continued to wait for the buck I was after to make his appearance. Twelve o'clock, one o'clock, and still no sighting of the buck I was after. He showed up the day before at 2 p.m., so I thought maybe he would do the same thing. There was almost non-stop action of animals but just not him. It's amazing how comfortable deer are when they don't sense any threat of danger.

I was pretty determined I was going to wait for this particular buck, and when the afternoon move started at around 3 p.m. I thought it was just a matter of time before the buck we called Droptine showed up. Pretty soon after, a small buck scared off the does from where they were feeding, and other bucks began to follow. It wasn't too long when that eight-point with three other smaller bucks came walking into the field. That eight-point kept tempting me, but I knew that if you want to shoot bigger, more mature bucks, sometimes you just have to wait it out. The eight-point with all the other bucks in the field that the big guy seemed to hang around with fed and walked around the field for nearly two hours. At one point, some did get a little spooky and started snorting, causing all the other deer to be on edge, and I thought, *well, there they all go, as all the deer started to exit the field.* After a short period of time, the eight-point, along with the other bucks, settled down and re-entered the field. Still no sign of the buck I was after.

As time was starting to wind down, I began to have doubts that drop tine would show up, and the next day, it was supposed to rain all day, and the wind direction would be going straight to where the deer fed out in the field. I wasn't sure what I was going to do. All day the wind had been perfect, blowing from the deer to me, and I didn't get winded the entire time. At about fifteen minutes of legal shooting light, suddenly, the noses of all the deer went straight up, and they began to smell something they didn't like. Then they got real fidgety and began to look in my direction as their body language was suddenly very tense. The gentle wind had swirled, and they got a whiff of me.

I had a split decision I had to make, and in seconds a ton of thoughts were going through my mind. Wife gone, and kids home alone, do I want to be gone another day? I sat all day with no food or water, hoping the big one would come. Do I want to do this again tomorrow and go hungry for twelve to fifteen hours with no food or water? Tomorrow, the weather is going to be terrible, and the wind direction will be wrong. Do I want to sit in the rain tomorrow because I can't sit in this blind with a roof? Do I want to eat tag soup and not get a deer in Ohio when I had put in a decent effort this past week to prepare for this hunt?

As I was contemplating all these thoughts running through my mind, the deer started to work their way towards the back of the field to leave. It was now or never. Was I going to settle for a much smaller buck or wait it out and hope that by some chance, the buck I was after would come in even though all the other deer were nervous? At the crack of the muzzleloader, the eight-point kicked and made a death run up into the woods where he fell over, kicking up a bunch of snow, and was expired in literal seconds.

I had made my decision hastily because I had no choice. I couldn't take back pulling the trigger. I couldn't decide it was a bad decision and changed my mind. I pulled the trigger on a mediocre buck, and it was lying dead in the woods. My Ohio deer tag was now filled. That entire day's sit came down to that one shot, and whether I liked it or not, it didn't change the outcome. I went over and immediately found the deer. Then I took all my stuff down the mountain and got the necessary equipment to get the deer out and went back up the mountain after him.

Thankfully the snow actually helped with the drag process, and by 9 p.m. I had dropped him off at the butcher, changed at a gas station, and was on my way home. Five-hour energy drinks do work, at least for me.

Did I make the right decision? I'm not entirely sure. But I made it, and when I see it hanging on my wall, I will relive the experience and re-weigh all the different reasons why I did what I did. And perhaps, over time, my opinion of my decision will change.

As I was walking down the mountain with my deer behind me, I was talking to the Lord and thanking Him that I even was in a position of health and strength on a beautiful piece of property, hunting the greatest animal on earth to where I had to make a hasty decision and consider the results later.

So, did I make the right decision? I think so because I did the best I could with what limited information I had. And that is all you can do. Incidentally, the buck I was after never showed up in front of the camera until 1 a.m. later that night, and I didn't get a picture of him at all the next few days. That helps some.

Do you have a decision to make that you don't have oodles of time to consider? You can't wring your hands over it for the rest of your life. Ask God for wisdom and make the best decision you can with what information you have, and go for it. You will have time to consider whether it was the right decision or not down the road. And even if the results aren't what you expected, it doesn't necessarily mean at the time of your decision that it was the wrong one. Maybe it was you just simply didn't have the right expectations.

"A man's heart plans his way, but the Lord directs his steps" (Proverbs 16:9).

REMEMBERING WHAT JESUS REALLY WENT THROUGH

It had been almost a month to the day that I had been up in a tree with a weapon chasing the elusive whitetail buck. I got up early on a Thursday morning and drove for five hours south to Southeast Ohio to put out a few bags of corn and a camera to see what was roaming the lease I had permission to hunt on in preparation for the upcoming muzzleloader season this coming weekend. I figured if I got there early enough and took care of business, I would bow hunt in a spot I had never hunted on the property and maybe end the season that way. It certainly would have been preferred. I took care of business and had a few hours to spare before I had to make the trip home. So I collected my hunting gear and headed to the tree.

As hunters, we will put up with a lot of inconveniences just for the opportunity at a mature buck. Just taking one hundred pounds of corn up a mountain, I thought it was going to give me a heart attack several times. I actually texted my wife, half-joking and half out of concern, because I couldn't get my heart rate to get back in line for a bit. Let's just say I settled for two bags versus the four I had planned. That might come back to haunt me this coming weekend.

What I seemed to forget through this whole process until I got to the area and was ready to climb up the tree was that about four days earlier, playing soccer in the basement in our socks with my boys and several other young people (I was the oldest by decades) I broke my big toe, or at least severely sprained it. In my zeal to score a stupid goal, I turned and kicked at the ball all in one motion from point-blank range, only to kick the teenage goalie square in the knee. I don't know if you are aware of this, but a knee is a much harder bone than a big toe. Needless to say, immediate throbbing pain. But after limping around for a bit, I finished the game and then later played around the world ping-pong. I have a hunch that playing those things afterward didn't help the situation.

But now I'm climbing up my tree with my climbing sticks, and I'm starting to feel the pain in my toe. I finished climbing the tree, got set up in my tree saddle system and platform, and with my mind temporarily off the pain in my toe, I began to look at the surroundings of where I chose to hunt. The land was stunning, right on the edge of a deep valley with a creek down at the bottom. Behind me was a power line where I could see hundreds of yards. I thought for sure I would at least see a deer, but amazingly, I got skunked.

The way you hunt from a tree saddle, you're pretty much leaning a little away from the tree the whole time. So there is constant pressure on your feet, with most of it being pushed towards the front, yes, towards the tips of your toes. Very soon after not seeing anything and waiting for a glimpse of a deer, the pain in my big toe began to remind me of what happened a few days earlier. Honestly, from there on out, I couldn't stand still. The pain was so irritating, with nothing to take my mind off of it. It didn't matter how much I moved or tried to adjust. My big fat toe just ached horribly.

As I kept trying to move around to find a place of relative comfort for Mr. Big, my mind went to Jesus on the cross. I began to remember that His feet were spiked to a cross, and the weight of His entire body rested on those spiked feet. Already His legs were so weak He could barely walk. Now He is having to rest all that weight on His feet. Suddenly the pain in my toe didn't seem quite that bad.

Have you ever thought about what Jesus went through? I don't mean dying on the cross. We so often generalize the cross as this big event, but we often don't consider the many details of the path to the cross and, of course, the actual hanging on the cross.

Immediately after His arrest, we see that He was punched and hit in the face and spit on. Shortly after that, He was whipped, which the way they whipped back then, the tool for punishment would rip the flesh off your back. I think the movie *The Passion of the Christ* by Mel Gibson does a pretty good job at showing what actually happened in a whipping. This happened twice to Him in a short period of time. Then He has a crown of thorns placed on His head and crushed down through the skin into His skull. Think of how being poked by just one needle feels. How about hundreds possibly at one time? His back is torn to shreds. His face is swollen and black and blue and now has blood running down His face from thorns sticking to His scalp. But His pain wasn't done.

They force Him to carry His own murder weapon across His mangled back to the hill He is to be killed on. He's so weak in His legs from the amount of blood He lost that He has no strength to carry on. It was those weak legs that He had to use to push Himself up on the cross just so He could breathe.

He finally makes it to His place of death by someone else, eventually carrying the cross He was too weak to carry. He's forced down on the cross as spikes are driven through His hands and through His feet. You can be sure these professional killers weren't careful like surgeons. Now Jesus is securely fastened to this cross, and the post dropped into place while He hangs there.

Now He is hanging there, and the way He hung on the cross, the only way He can breathe is to prop Himself up, putting pressure on the feet spiked to the cross using His exhausted legs. After the pain was so excruciating and the strength in His legs gone, He would sink down and immediately not be able to breathe until He could lift Himself up again, just long enough to gasp for some breath. Of course, lifting Himself enough to breathe would cause Him to scrape the mangled open flesh of His back on the cross. From the base of the feet of Jesus to the top of His head, He was beaten, bloodied, bruised, and His body mangled. The Bible says that His appearance changed so much He was not recognizable.

The real death of Christ was so much more than a polite image of Jesus hanging on a cross with a little bit of blood coming out from His pierced hands and feet.

Suddenly, my achy toe didn't hurt quite so badly. Just remember that the next time Christ asks something of you for Himself. He just didn't die for you. He embraced intense agony and pain through the entire process with finally the rejection of His Own Father for a time because He became sin, for you, for me. He took upon Himself the sin of the whole world. Every act of hate, immorality, homosexuality, murder, lie, lustful thought, rebellious act, pride, and self-will... Then, He died.

If you ever want a glimpse of how evil your heart is without Christ, just think of how you so often act out in a way that displeases Him. Yea, me too! After all He has done, it's hard to comprehend the depravity of every one of us. And yet He is patient and willingly forgives us.

I hope this simple devotional, inspired by a busted-up toe, gives you a heightened appreciation for everything Jesus endured for you. Nothing has happened like it in history, before, or since. There is only one person who cared enough for you and for me that 2,000 years before we lived... He died.

WITH A PERFECT HEART

In 2 Kings 22:2, He (speaking of King Josiah, who was eight years old by the way when he began to reign) did what was right in the eyes of the Lord and followed completely the ways of his father, David, not turning aside to the right or to the left.

One of the things you will notice when you read the book of 2 Kings in regards specifically to the kings of Judah was that many of them "did what was right" in the sight of the Lord, but "not with a perfect heart." Israel, on the other hand, pretty much had all wicked kings from the time that the kingdom separated after Solomon's reign, with Jeroboam being Israel's first king. But most of Judah's kings served the Lord to some capacity, and their reigns were always compared to that of King David's due to David, even with great failure, never once walked away from serving the Lord. King David pleased God so much that he became the standard by which every other king of Judah was judged. Either the kings walked in the ways of their father David, or they walked in the ways of their father David but not with a perfect heart (most kings of Judah), or they didn't walk in the ways of their father David and did evil in the sight of the Lord. Those were pretty much the three scenarios with the kings of Judah. Again, Israel just blew it right from the separation of the nation as a whole and literally just went down the road of false idols from then on out. Hard to believe not a single king of Israel served God, which is why they were destroyed before Judah. God's patience ran out, and they were wiped out.

Judah wasn't innocent either, and their day came when they were taken captive. But not before Josiah. He was one of the last legitimate Godly kings of Israel. The part that caught my attention about Josiah is where it says he didn't turn from the right or to the left. He followed "completely" the ways of his father, David. He didn't turn but stayed on the straight and narrow path... *all*... his days.

When I heard that read on my Bible app, it really stuck out to me and convicted my heart. These stories are here not just to give a history of Israel, but for us to learn the truths in every story that are both staring us in the face and some that are more hidden and yet still there, and often the hidden ones are some of the most important.

When I heard that verse read aloud on my Bible app, I could have gone back and remembered all the times when maybe I did get distracted or turned to the right or the left. Nope, I've never not served the Lord since I gave my life to Christ as a five-year-old, like many of the kings of Judah, but not with a perfect heart, again, like many of the kings of Judah. But instead of looking back and sorrowing over the times I may have strayed, I looked forward, and the desire and prayer of my heart were, "Lord, I don't want to turn to the right or to the left in my life. I don't want to stray from the path of following you!"

Those who love the great hymns of the faith, as I do know the verse in the one hymn that says, "Prone to wander Lord I feel it, prone to leave the God I love!" While I am prone to that type of lifestyle, I don't want that to be my testimony. I want every fiber of my life to become more in tune with the ways of God. I want the character of God to become more evident in my life and so much less of me that shows. I want the desire for the ways of God to be so ingrained in my life that the slightest appearance of the world disappears at the brightness of the light of Christ showing through me. I want *nothing* in my life to replicate the appearance of this world system from attitudes, actions, thoughts, my language, and definitely not my desires. I have a *long* way to go, and I know it. But it's His work. My responsibility is to surrender to the Potter's wheel.

The Lord knows there are plenty of things to cause us to turn to the right or to the left. If King Solomon could fall into that category, who do I think I am to think I do not run the same risk of slipping onto another path that slowly leads away from the straight and "narrow" path?

There is a way to secure our lives from straying off the narrow path we are called to walk. It's the second part of the verse to that great hymn, "Here's my heart Lord, take and seal it, seal it for thy courts above." A surrendered heart to the Lord with a humble prayer that asks the Lord to seal our hearts (your will, your desires, your thoughts, your plans) to Him, for His honor and His plans and for His kingdom's sake. After all, in the end, everything else is temporal and doesn't matter.

If that is our heart's desire, our testimony can be like King Josiah's, that we didn't turn to the right or to the left all of our days. And the beautiful thing is, if that *is* our testimony as of right now, we can change our story. Today we can get back on the straight and narrow path and never leave again because we don't mourn over what hasn't been but rejoice in what can be.

Philippians 3:13:

Brethren, I count not myself to have apprehended: but this one thing I do, forgetting those things which are behind, and reaching forth unto those things which are before, I press toward the mark for the prize of the high calling of God in Christ Jesus.

BE CAREFUL WHAT YOU SAY YOU HATE

Ever say you hate something only for it to save your bacon later on?

I have this carabiner "S" hook with latches on each side that is big and bulky, and what I was using it for just wasn't working. I had taken off one of the clips, so one side was always open. The other day I audibly said to myself as I put it in the backpack never to be used again, that I hated that thing.

I was hunting in Southern Ohio a couple of weeks later and have this new system of climbing that I am trying out for my particular style of hunting. I got to the tree, set up my climbing system, attached the carabiner on my pull rope to my camera arm, orange jacket, and gun, and finally to my saddle loop so I could just pull it all up when I got up to the height I wanted.

I started my climb, and I got about seventeen feet high and figured that was plenty because I was actually looking down into the valley. I took my backpack off, strapped it to the tree, and attached my camera arm to the tree so when I pulled my camera arm up, I could just attach the camera and would be ready to go, everything was going great until I started to pull up my rope and the gun slid off the coat to the ground. Somehow I forgot to clip the gun in as well. I pulled up my coat and camera, set up my camera, and figured I would climb back down, attach the gun, climb back up, and then everything would be fine. Until that is, I went to grab the loose dangling end of my tree tether to loosen it some more, only to find out it was between the extremely tight strap of my camera arm and the tree. I would have to take off the camera, take off the camera arm, loosen the camera brace, get my rope out, re-secure the camera bracket, put the camera arm back on, then install the camera, then climb down the tree, attach my gun to the pull rope and climb back up. I'm tired of just thinking about it.

As I'm sitting there thinking about what I am going to do, I remember the "S" hook carabiner. So, I pull that out, clip it onto the other carabiner on the pull rope... lower it down, and with the open side of the "S" hook, I slowly drag it across the shoulder strap of my firearm that is laying on the ground. Unbelievably, it only took maybe three tries, and the hook snagged the shoulder strap, and I pulled my gun up.

Have I ever told you how much I *love* that silly... I mean... awesome "S" hook carabiner? It's one of my new favorite pieces of hunting equipment!

I've been there and done that with people. Not only due to their personality trait that I just didn't really like or because I thought they didn't have the necessary capabilities that I expected in them. And certainly, there are people that we will never gel with or don't have the talents that we may need for a particular job we are doing. But like that "S" hook, there have been times where I have had to change my perspective and realize that I was wrong about them, and I could actually use them in a particular area that I needed. In fact, sometimes, they had been super helpful in ways that I would have been in trouble had I not had them around at the time to be able to utilize their abilities.

And "S" hook is one thing. But people are much more valuable and have to be cared for and handled much differently. One of the often tough responsibilities of a leader is to find out where a person best fits versus just writing them off. A good leader will exhaust every possibility before he realizes they just aren't a good fit. And sometimes, in that process of evaluating, he will find that they actually have a perfect place in his system of leadership.

Because of the value of people, I want to be very slow to write anyone off. And even if they may not be a good fit for my life, I don't want to just cast them off to the side. I would think a much better option would be to carefully, graciously help them find a good fit for them. Every person has a place and a perfect use if they are willing to try their best. And sometimes that may be to help you get out of an unexpected dilemma.

The moral of the story: be careful what you say you hate! They, it, or that "thing" might save your bacon one day. It's all about perspective!

LET THE LORD WHITTLE AWAY

What I learned from a potato:

It was my oldest daughter's birthday, and naturally, when it's that time of year, usually her sister, a couple of friends, her mom, and she will want to go shopping. That left me at home with the boys to put her gift together. I also was given detailed instructions on what to do with the chicken my wife had prepared for that night's dinner. One of my daughter's favorite meals is breaded chicken and mashed potatoes. My wife makes absolutely the best mashed potatoes. They don't seem hard to make, as I have helped her several times. But hers are just better than everyone else's. Along with instructions for chicken, I was asked to peel the taters and put them in a pan with water at the prescribed time; when they left from their conquest of emptying their wallets at the mall, as usual, they did a pretty good job.

I was given the go-ahead to get moving on the peeling, so I grabbed a half-full 5lb bag and started peeling. For each potato, I would carefully start on one side, work my way around and then turn it around and do the other side. Once I was done, I would wash the potato in water and then carefully inspect it for any imperfections. That potato was not set aside to work on another one until, upon inspection, every blemish was peeled off. Mashed potatoes can be really good, just like any food, if quality matters, and you make them with a little TLC. When I was done, there were about twenty potatoes all ready to be chopped up and put in the pan to boil until soft. Once that is done, they are mashed, and I mean mashed, none of that chunk nonsense! Ours go down the old food pipe smooth! Once they are mashed nice and smooth, my wife begins to add the ingredients until they are ready to be taste tested. I am the official taste-tester. Being the taste tester has caused me a lot of extra pounds. At least that's my story, and I'm sticking to it.

As I meticulously peeled those potatoes, some of the blemishes ran deep. And I would keep peeling and peeling until all that was showing was the white of the potato. One potato, in fact, the blemish ran all the way through, and I couldn't use it! It was separated from the others and thrown into the garbage.

If you were paying attention at all to what I have written so far, you might have seen there are several lessons that can be learned, but I am going to focus on just one.

Right now, I feel like a potato where the Lord is carefully and meticulously peeling away the hard surface of who I am. Why? Because He has a plan for what I am supposed to be and, if I may, how I am to be used to feed the body of Christ. Every stroke away from that surface is painful, but not one of them is a waste. And here is the kicker, once everything looks good at a glance, often, upon careful inspection, there is a blemish that runs deeper and needs to be worked out. More time in the prep process. And, of course, the deeper He cuts, the more painful it is.

You might be asking, what is so encouraging about that? Well, God is the master chef. He's gentle. He's patient. He pours grace over you with every stroke of His peeler. And best of all, He is making you into something that is unique and one of a kind—His own masterpiece.

It's taking too long! Do you want Him to stop and not finish perfecting you? He needs to go faster! Are you sure you want Him to do that? How often can we barely handle the refining now? No, we just need to trust God! That is true rest when you just let go of fighting and let God do His thing!

Lesson number one of the potato: Embrace the process! It's leading to a good result in you and through you!

LIVE IN THE AUDIENCE OF ONE

As someone who watches a fair amount of YouTube, mainly Christian music, sermons, hunting, or to find out how to do something, one thing that has always amazed me is that upon watching an excellent video in any category, there are always dislikes, sometimes several hundred! Sometimes, I will be sitting there with tears in my eyes for a guy who just missed a giant buck. Oh wait, that was a video of me. Or some preacher speaks an excellent message, again tears. Some singer performs world-class song. Some guy has one of the most amazing experiences ever, and the list goes on and on, and there will *always,* without exception, be some thumbs down. Someone, or usually multiple someones, will dislike the video. You get over 10,000 views on a video, which I've not had to worry about yet, and there will inevitably be some dislikes. It never ceases to amaze me.

My small engine mechanics teacher back in school decades ago now used to say to our class, "You can please all the people half the time, or half the people all the time." He was more right than I gave him credit for back then. The reality is, though, that you will *never* please everyone; not going to happen. There will always be someone at some point who is not happy with you for something you did. Let's face it. We often give plenty of reasons for people not to be happy with us. But even if we were perfect, it still wouldn't matter. I can prove that is the truth in one word: Jesus! Lived a perfect, sinless life. Died on the cross for every sinner that ever lived, and yet to this day, people are not happy about His existence.

So, if you cannot always make everyone happy all the time, what then is the answer? Well, really, it's quite simple. Do what Jesus did. Live in the audience of one! Jesus said that He literally only did whatever He saw His Father do. He kept His attention on what His Father was doing, and He mirrored what He saw. Nothing more, nothing less. That's all we have to do as well. Live in the Audience of One. Notice the capital "O"? Because you always capitalize the first letter when referring to deity. Yes, that "One" is Jesus. When all is said and done, there should be only One person we are trying to mirror. Our actions and words should show a healthy fear of Him. Our attempts to spend time with Him and meditate on Him and talk to Him should show our deepening love for Him and recognition of His love for us. If we are seeking to please Him. (The Bible says, if you are not surrendered to the Lordship of Christ, you are abiding under His wrath. But no one has to remain in that condition). The way we treat our wives, husbands, sons, daughters, brothers and sisters, friends, and foes should be our best attempt at mirroring what we see Jesus do in the Bible. Everything we try to do and everything we don't do should be a direct result that we are only concerned about living in His audience. If you do that, most definitely, you are not going to make everyone happy. Actually, according to the Bible, you will most likely have more against you than for you. But if the audience you are focused on is Jesus, no one else really matters. If everyone else matters and Jesus means very little as your audience, then you are focused on the wrong people and setting yourself up for disappointment, both in this life and the next. And the worst part of being in that spot is that the most important person in the universe that should be happy with us isn't. He will be displeased with our lives because we chose to please man instead of God.

You and I are going to have enemies. The question is, who are they going to be? The audience that you are seeking to please will determine who those enemies are and who your friends are.

It might not be a bad idea to do a little self-search to see who your main audience is that you're catering to. The easiest way to tell is, which way are you being pulled? Do you slide towards the ways and pressures of this sinful world when around ungodly people? Or, when you are around them, are they careful about how they live and act and what they say? Jesus had no problem being around the wicked, whether religious or ungodly. But they were drawn to Him, not Him to them.

If we live in the audience of One, one thing is for sure. We will reflect the light of the "Son" to those around us. And let's be honest, aside from ultimately being here to bring God pleasure, being a light in this world is the second most important reason we are here. First—love God, second—love people. That can only *truly* happen when we live in the audience of One. And that One is Jesus!

THE STORIES IN THE BIBLE REALLY HAPPENED—PASS IT ON

I was in the basement of a client of ours that we had serviced for nearly ten years. His basement had flooded with the monsoon rains we had that particular summer, and so I was there with the carpet guy as he measured up for all the carpet replacement that needed to be done. It was taking him a rather long time to make sure he got everything correct. So while he was measuring, I was just kind of walking around.

As I said, I had known this family for nearly ten years, and while they are nice people, they clearly were not Christians, nor did they make any attempts for you to believe that they were. Never once have I ever needed to discern their position when it came to Christianity.

As I was walking around in the kids' playroom, I noticed a bookcase filled with kids' books on it. I walked over to it and was staring at the titles, some popular fairy tale books and some fiction books like *Cinderella, The Smurfs, Robin Hood, Stories in the Bible, Billy And The Timber Rattler,* and *Where The Red Fern Grows.*

See what I did there? A bunch of kids' fairytale and fictional books there, and sandwiched right in the middle was a book about stories of the Bible. I really wonder, first of all, if that boy ever read about those stories, and if he did, does he think they are just another group of fairy tales and fictional stories that were made up? Based on what I know about the family, I would have to assume he does.

I certainly have no problem with a kids' book about the stories in the Bible to make it somewhat understandable for kids, but we must never allow our children or anyone we know, including the unsaved, to think that the characters in the Bible were fictional characters only to fill the pages of a book we call the Bible. Even as we teach them at a child's level, they *must know* these were real people who did extraordinary things, some good and some bad. David was a real shepherd. He really slew a giant with a sling and then chopped off his head with a sword (no pictures necessary). Joseph was a real boy who was sold into slavery by his own brothers and literally ended up saving the whole world by being the ruler of Egypt, second only to Pharaoh. Esther really was a young niece to her uncle Mordecai and literally became the queen of the most powerful king in the world at that time. She really risked her neck to save her own people, and save them she did! Then, of course, there is Mary, the young virgin who was minding her own business, excited about the upcoming marriage to Joseph, and the angel Gabriel came and messed up all their plans by, oh, I don't know, letting her know she was going to carry the son of God in her stomach for nine months when she had never known a man. And she accepted the responsibility to raise the Son of God, to breastfeed Him, change His diapers, clean His clothes, Cut His hair and watch Him die on a cross. Yes, die on a cross. Jesus died on a cross, and even more amazing perhaps than that, He rose again. It's one of the most documented events in history, and yet, so often, it's relayed almost as if it were a fairytale.

Moses spoke to God at a Burning bush. God parted the Red Sea. He destroyed the entire Egyptian army, including Pharaoh, in that sea (sorry, Charlton Heston and Hollywood, you still played a killer Moses, though). Peter and Paul really healed people by the power of the Holy Spirit.

Our children *have* to *know* and *believe* these things *really* happened, and so do we! By not teaching them that the Bible is true and these things happened, you rob them of so many important truths that they need to know, so they can live according to those truths. But perhaps the most important of those truths that they are missing if they don't believe the stories are real are:

1. The Bible points to the Living God. The God of the Bible is real.

2. God truly is sovereign—He has been and will always be in control, and in the chaos of this world, they need to know that things are not happening at a random chance, both on the world stage but also on a personal level in each of our lives. He is our shepherd, and He leads us.

3. If you learn to know the God of the Bible, you can do extraordinary things as well! Elisha was a man "subject to like passions" as we are, but he was a man used by God in incredible ways. We need some young people to stand up and be used by God in our society and country. Seeing what fallible sinful men and women were capable of when they trusted in God will give them the faith in God that they too can be used in exceptional ways. But perhaps just as important is someone used in an amazing way is a whole group of young people that grow up and follow Christ and raise their kids to follow Christ. Whether doing great things or doing spiritual "mundane" things faithfully, we all have a part to play in advancing God's kingdom.

4. Last but certainly not least. God has always shown an amazing desire for a relationship with his creation. When you read the true stories of the Bible, you can't help but see God was always involved with His people corporately and individually for those who wanted to know Him. He was always looking for a relationship. From walking with Adam and Eve in the Cool of the Garden to showing John the Beloved how one day He is going to create a new heaven and a new earth, and heaven is going to come down to earth, and God is going to dwell with us forever. Now that *sounds* like a fairytale, but it's not. It's all true. And if we don't make a point to read these stories and teach them to our kids, and preach them to our friends, saved and unsaved, along with the truths that each story has for us, our book of the stories in the Bible will end up collecting dust on some shelf with all the rest of the fairytale stories. And by the time our kids are grown, they won't know the difference between David killing Goliath and *Beauty and the Beast*... and we may not either.

SHOW PATIENCE—YOU'LL NEED IT SHOWN TO YOU ONE DAY

Ever have to eat humble pie, even when no one else knows it? I was waiting at Sam's gas station to fill up the tank, and as usual, it was fairly busy. There were a couple of ladies in front of me pumping gas. The one in the front got done relatively quickly and drove off. Just as she drove off, the older lady in the back finished pumping her gas and put the pump back and stood there, not sure what to do next, apparently. I figured I would wait until she left, then I would drive up to the front pump. She stood there for some time, presumably waiting for a receipt, and then she got into her vehicle. That seemed to take much longer, in my opinion, than it should have with a couple of people waiting for her, but eventually, she started the car and drove off. As I pulled up, I said to myself in my mind, "Well, Phil, you just need to show her a little patience." The clear thought in my heart at the moment, almost subconsciously, was that I needed to show her patience because she was just not as good or smooth as me when it came to doing these things. Quite arrogant, actually. But though ashamed to say that it was, in fact, my attitude.

As she drove off, I pulled up to the farthest pump so the lady who had also been waiting behind me could also get to the back pump. I hopped out in a hurry because now two other cars had pulled up and were waiting. I slipped my Sam's card in and waited for the next step… nothing… Hmmm… So I slid the card in again and quickly pulled it out… Nothing… What is going on? So then I thought maybe I misunderstood the steps even though I've done it a thousand times before, so I slipped in my credit card, and it held onto it for a few seconds as it always does, then read, "Do not recognize club membership card." Now I'm getting really irritated. I've done this so many times. It's literally just natural. I have a system, and the system never fails. I'm usually in and out as fast as you can be when filling up a truck's gas tank. The lady behind me is already done pumping, and I haven't even started yet. I turn the membership card over, thinking maybe the black stripe is getting worn down, only to realize I have been sliding the card in the wrong way every time. The black stripe was supposed to be on the right, and I was sliding it in on the left.

Just as fast as I realized what I had done, the thought came to me, *The reason you needed to show patience to that lady in front of you was not that you were better than her, but rather because you're just like her and you need others to show you patience just as much as you needed to show that lady patience!*

The whole foundation of why I thought I needed to show that lady patience was completely wrong, rooted entirely out of pride. I am often reminded of what God says when it comes to His way of judging man: Man looks on the outward appearance, but God looks at the heart! I acted, to myself, all smug and patient with that poor lady, and yet it was entirely stinky and displeasing to the Lord. I needed to be humbled... and it didn't take long.

Just two quick things to remember and learn from my stupidity. It doesn't matter how good your actions look. God is investigating the motive... as the Bible says, "The thoughts and intents of the heart" are the things that really matter to Him. Pretty or handsome on the outside doesn't mean anything to Him if the heart is rotten. In fact, for many, beauty on the outside is a curse. It has ruined countless people. Some of which I know, unfortunately. But money can be the same way. You see rich people giving thousands of dollars to this charity or that charity. And the obvious response for most is to be so impressed. Only to find out if you really knew the motive was that they had to give money away to charity for tax purposes. Again, man is looking at the outward appearance, and God is looking at the heart. Over my lifetime, I have seen so many things that looked so good on the outside, only to realize later there was a ridiculously selfish hidden motive. But not to get too critical, this story started with me doing the same thing or revealing the same thing about my heart. My pious patience was nothing more than arrogant self-righteousness.

Second. The next time you are struggling to show patience to someone who legitimately needs it, you're doing it not because you're better but rather because your time is coming, and you will need someone's patience for yourself. I am quite confident I have needed others' patience much more than I needed to give it

Truly, patience is a virtue!

GOD WILL NOT WASTE
YOUR SERVICE

Does the church you go to ever have church work days? Ever since I was a boy, whether chopping wood in the fall on Saturday when I wanted to be hunting or working at the present church painting or cleaning something, the churches I have always attended have had church work days. There aren't too many per year, but many hands do make light work, and it's a good time to serve the body of Christ as a group.

There was this one particular work day that left an impression on me. I was working with a group of men cleaning out church items in a building our church owns. Technically nothing was supposed to be stored in this building, and yet it was full of VBS decorations from years past. I think there were two old organs we threw out with a myriad of other things. We ordered two thirty-yard dumpsters and, within just a couple of hours, had them filled to overflowing. And yet there were a lot of things still left to throw out, so we scheduled another day to remove the rest.

While I was cleaning out the area I was working in, I came across several boxes like what I have pictured in this post. They were above my head, so I was not sure what they even were or how heavy they were, seeing they were decorated boxes. When I grabbed a hold of one to pull it and realized it was super light, I opened the lid only to find out that it was just a cardboard box. I can't explain why, and who can tell why one thing affects us over another, but my eyes immediately filled up with tears. I was looking at a box decorated so well that when it was above my head, I didn't even realize it was a cardboard box. And there were several of these items, more of these decorated cardboard boxes, huge wooden stairs built with incredible decorations and canvas paintings, paper crafted animals, and the amount of constructed pieces of everything you could imagine were laying there just waiting to be thrown in the garbage. Within just a couple of hours, almost all of it was broken and carefully stacked into two dumpsters. All told, those dumpsters represented thousands of hours of people laboring, young and old, because they loved children and wanted to have a positive effect on the lives of these kids, many they didn't even know.

I quietly hid my tears as everyone was faithfully working and cleaning. It's amazing how quickly things can be destroyed. But you know what? Just because those things were torn down and discarded so fast into a dumpster doesn't mean they didn't have the desired effect it was supposed to have, a lasting, eternal impact.

I will never forget sitting in the back of the church sanctuary for the final day of VBS one year as my brother, who was the leader of the entire Vacation Bible School, gave a message of salvation to probably 250 people of all ages. Fathers, mothers, sons and daughters, single men and women, all sitting there as my brother gave one of the most powerful salvation messages you could have heard. I wanted to give my life to Christ all over again.

At the end of the message, he asked for everyone to bow their heads and close their eyes, and if they wanted to surrender to Christ as their Savior, to raise their hand. I cheated and kept my eyes open to see what would happen. About twenty-seven people raised their hands that night to give their lives to Christ, including one fairly rough-looking man sitting right in front of me. I will never forget that tattooed arm being raised to heaven as he accepted Christ. That man and I are now great friends, and He is a phenomenal example of how God can change anyone's life who will let Him have control.

Those boxes worked, after all. All those decorations sitting in that garbage heap did what they were intended to do. Be a labor of love to bring people to a place where they can hear what truly matters in life. And everyone who gave of their free time so willingly will not even know the full extent of the impact they had on these kids until they get to heaven and see what God really thought of their efforts.

Maybe that's how you feel in your life. You have invested your life into people, trying to do your best to be a blessing to those around you and possibly to those you don't even know. Maybe you haven't seen almost any benefit from your efforts. Maybe you are older now, and it "appears" that your efforts to help others have been for no lasting purpose. Our labor of love may vanish over time in your own mind or the minds of those around us, but God does not forget. Your kindness, love, and helping hand is never in vain.

Just like that box that was crushed and thrown away in the garbage, our lives are only here for a time, and then, like everyone before us, we meet our ultimate resting place. It's only after we die that our true usefulness will be recognized. Because what others often miss, God never does. He always sees what everyone else misses!

Remember, Jesus said it was the person hiding in their closet doing what they were supposed to be doing that no one saw until God rewarded them openly. Your service is laying up for yourself treasures in heaven where moth and rust and a bunch of men on a church work day can't destroy.

"But lay up for yourselves treasures in heaven, where neither moth nor rust doth corrupt, and where thieves do not break through nor steal" (Matthew 6:20).

THE MASTER'S HAND GIVES YOU VALUE

That... thing... in the picture looks stupid and useless, doesn't it? About eighteen or nineteen years ago, the company I work for was doing a massive remodeling project which included two additions to add to an already very big house. What was supposed to be one addition turned into two, and then eventually, every bit of the house was gutted down to wood studs.

We had hired painters to do the painting instead of our company, but their quality was just not up to our standards. So we decided we would let them paint the walls and ceiling, but we would do all the trim and any artistic finishes. The clients had a designer who was in charge of every detail of how the house was going to look, and she would often have some pretty crazy ideas. One time she handed me a piece of trim that was multi-colored, with some of the colors being very faint, and said she wanted all the trim in the entire den to match that piece of wood. I spent an entire week figuring out how to match that piece of trim exactly. I came back one morning after leaving a sample to dry overnight, only to find all the paint had peeled up from the board. I did figure it out eventually, and to this day, their den trim is painted with the finished product.

Another time the designer walked into the house while we were working. She handed me a piece of leather and told me she wanted all the trim and wood parts of the seats in the theater room in the basement to match that piece of leather material... with paint. Oh, okay, yeah, let me just whip something up here in about twenty seconds because this one's a piece of cake. Yea right. Off to the drawing board. It didn't actually take me that long to figure out the multi-tone of colors in that piece of leather. The hard part was replicating the texture of the leather with paint. I spent many hours trying different tools and brushes and almost everything I could think of. But nothing worked. One day I was collaborating with my cousin/boss about it, and I thought maybe a piece of rope could somehow work. He thought maybe to fray the edges and see if that helped. Shockingly, it looked amazingly similar to what we were trying to replicate. We had found our tool. Now I just had to make it into something usable so we could do the 10,000 dollars paint job on just the trim.

One of the strengths of my father was that he was an inventor. He could create some of the craziest things for whatever he needed. Somehow I got that creative gene to try and make stuff out of seemingly nothing. Well, as you see in the picture, that's what I created. A rope wrapped by a couple of artists' brushes is tied together, with the rope being frayed at the end. I can't tell you how good that job came out. And the designer and client were both quite pleased with the finished product that I and my cousin had done. We had created a masterpiece with a piece of junk good-for-nothing rope that was lying around.

I bet without any explanation, most everyone would look at that brush and laugh and think that contraption is probably useful for nothing. And they would be right. That brush has sat in our paint trailer for the last eighteen years or so and has never been used again. Essentially completely worthless, except for the occasional reminiscing.

What made that brush worth anything was the master's hand that was guiding it and carefully brushing across the freshly applied paint to get the perfect look of what we were trying to replicate. That brush had no ability on its own. It didn't create itself, and it certainly didn't create the artistic finish. No, the masterpiece was created by the master's hand that understood he could create value and purpose for that brush.

Three quick points:

1. Apart from Christ, who is the master hand guiding your life, your life and my life are literally as useless as that silly brush without the ability of the painter. If you want something of importance to come from your life, let the master painter take control of the silly-looking, worthless-looking brush called your life. Only God can make something useful and eternal with so little. It all comes down to God, the Master Painter.

2. Before you were born, He had an intentional purpose for your life to create a masterpiece using you as His silly-looking brush. He intends for you to leave your mark on this earth, but doing it His way. Remember, the quality of the paint job was not because of the brush but because of the master painter using it. And He knew what the picture was supposed to look like before He started. Once again, it comes down to God and His Painting.

3. Oftentimes, you may feel, and I have certainly felt, like that brush looks stupid, of no value, and good for nothing. Don't ever forget, the Master Painter delights in using out-of-the-ordinary brushes to create His masterpiece. That's what makes Him exceptional. He uses the cheapest, dirtiest, stiffest brushes, and His paintings turn out by far the best. You just have to let him control the movements and pressure on the canvas. Your value is not in your beauty or ability but in your surrender of control. And one last time... it once again comes down to God, the Master Painter.

What will the brush say to the painter? Look what a great painting I have created! I dare say not!

By the way, I was not the "master" painter who used that brush. It was my cousin.

ENJOY MAKING THE MEMORY

For me, hunting is a lot like this picture. Clearly, this picture is *far* from the best drawing I've ever done and certainly ever seen. I have a couple of friends that if you didn't know they drew the picture, you would think it was a black and white photo. Incredible detail, far beyond my capabilities! I used to think I could draw until I saw their pictures. Then I realized I just scribbled. But you see, that doesn't matter in this picture. What makes this picture special is not the fact that it's so good. It's not. What makes it special is the memory I had of drawing it. Me and my friend on a school bus one day on the way home from school twenty-eight years ago, taking turns adding our own little touches of artistry to my lined piece of school paper. If you notice, on the bottom right-hand corner, it says *Matt and Phil 2/10/93*. Actually, on my birthday. See, the value of this picture is not in the quality but rather in the memory.

Deer hunting for me is just like that. I look around and see giant bucks being shot, and I end up with respectable bucks. In my hunting world, someone will always shoot a bigger buck, usually my hunting buddies. But that doesn't mean their hunts are any better or more fulfilling than mine. Every set of antlers I have, big or small, represents an incredible memory that the majority of the people in our country, let alone the world, never get to experience. A story of hard knocks leading to success, hard work, intense moments, cold and wet hours on the stand, adrenaline rushes that can't be matched by any other activity in life, hugs from brothers and cousins, celebrating with fathers and friends who have now passed on.

I have shot everything from a one-horn, barely legal buck to a ten-point 150-inch class buck, and I have to ask myself, *was I really more excited when I shot my biggest buck than I was when I shot my smallest buck?* Honestly, no. And every buck in between was the same adrenaline rush and shaky legs and hands, stumbling over words because I was drunk with the thrill of the chase and kill. No, every buck I have ever killed is not special because of the size of the rack. It's valuable because there is a memory attached to it. Every shoulder mount and European skull mount I have serves to remind me of the memory, the experience that was permanently etched into my brain like a file on a computer, to pull up and revisit and reminisce at the sight of each set of antlers. Sure, I admire the antlers, but that's short-lived as I quickly move to the memory of the experience I had. You know how I know that to be true? Whether it's a giant buck, a medium buck, or a small buck, when you first lay eyes on someone's prized trophy, it's only a matter of seconds before the hunter starts telling you about... the experience.

Just remember next time you're out there in the woods sitting in a tree or up against the base of a tree. It's not really a giant buck you're chasing. It's the desire for another experience and creating another memory that is driving you.

That same principle holds true with people as well. It's not about the size of the vacation, the size of the car you have, or the house you live in. No, it's the memories you make with the people that you are with and love. Give me a hut with a family that loves one another and enjoys each other's company, and I will take that any day over a mansion where the family is separated and barely around each other to experience the thrill and excitement of one another. Houses, money, and selfish pleasures come and go. But it's the experiences made with loved ones that are remembered and enjoyed.

Oftentimes we can work so hard trying to make something perfect that we miss the actual moment and never appreciate what we just experienced. I feel like with my children. I have done a fairly good job at not missing the moments because I was too busy trying to do something perfectly or got distracted with things that were "more important." I have caught most of the funny faces, misused words, silly jokes, or comedic actions that they have done over the years, at least when I was around them because I tried to relish the moment. It didn't matter that we may have been at the small kitchen table in a small house or out for ice cream instead of at a hotel. I cherished my children, and they made the memory, not where we were or what we wished we could have done.

When you are with loved ones, family or friends, learn to enjoy the experience and make the memory. Because ten years from now or much sooner, even if the situation wasn't the best, you will laugh at it because the part that you will remember was the people you were with.

DON'T FORGET TO KEEP GOD INVOLVED

It was a Sunday afternoon when our church had its annual memorial day picnic. The weather was perfect, and the time together with the church family was refreshing. We have a pavilion that you can sit under where the food and drinks are kept. About 150 yards away is where we play soccer. Usually, due to many injuries, I do my best to maintain self-control and not get involved lest I hurt myself again. I have a torn left chest muscle that never was fixed from a soccer game. I have torn my quad twice, and there is a bump in my leg where it is supposedly healed. A torn rotator cuff, ankle sprains, hamstrings, and other injuries just by forgetting I'm not twenty years old anymore. But the weather was too nice, and I was anxious to show the youngins I wasn't completely washed up. The good news is that I didn't get hurt. The bad news is that everything except the fingers I am writing with hurt and were sore. But pain is a good sign that exercise did what it was supposed to do. That's another story for another day.

In the process of playing soccer, there was a young father there who had taken off his shoes to play and put his keys in his shoes so he wouldn't lose them. Or so he thought. The truth was that while he thought that was what he did, he actually hadn't, and he was running around with keys in his pocket until they weren't. Of course, he didn't know that and continued to play. After the game was over, we all went back to the pavilion, got drinks, sat around, and eventually got ready to leave. That was when this father realized he did not have his keys. Naturally, with something being lost, I felt the need to help though I also felt like I could barely walk. I dragged my daughter along with me as she and I teased back and forth about who was the best at finding lost things. She was willing to relinquish the title at that moment as long as she didn't have to get up and help. But I didn't let her get out of it that easily. The three of us looked quite extensively everywhere we could think of, all around the pavilion, all around the soccer field, and where the spectators were watching/mocking us... nothing! Unfortunately, the grass was tall, so finding anything in it would be difficult, and we had come up empty. To be honest, we weren't even totally sure we were looking in the right place.

The dad went back to the pavilion, and my daughter and I looked a little more and didn't find anything. We were walking back to the pavilion when we met with the dad, and I asked him to retrace his steps for me. He thought for a minute and started telling me what he thought had happened, but there was clearly some confusion as to what he actually did. As he was telling me what he remembered, he abruptly stopped and asked me and my daughter if he could pray. We said, of course. I try to pray all the time when I am looking for something, and I had said a silent prayer already in my head. But he wanted to pray with us, so we naturally agreed. We closed our eyes, and he said a simple prayer request and, near the end, asked the Lord that if it's His will that He would help us find the missing keys quickly. After he prayed, he said amen, and my daughter and I both said amen agreeing with him. We turned and started walking back toward the soccer field, which was over a little knoll. We got about twenty yards into our journey back over there, and this little girl with her father came walking over the knoll toward us. The little girl held up a small set of keys and asked the father if they were his. That is about as quick of an answered prayer as you can get. He was, of course, incredibly relieved, and we were quite amazed at how fast, after a simple prayer, the keys showed up. The girl and her dad were over near the field, kicking a basketball around as if it was a soccer ball. Apparently, somehow, they heard we were looking for some keys, and she "happened" to stumble on them while they were kicking the ball around. Not a single one of us could puff out our chest, saying we found them. Nope, the Lord answered the prayer through a little girl we didn't even know. It's always better that way.

There are so many things I could point out about this scenario that are quite amazing. But there are only two thoughts I would like to mention if you will indulge me a couple more minutes of your time.

One, it's often difficult to pray because the feeling can be at times that God is so far away. And even if He does hear, the time it would/could take to answer a prayer leaves us doubting it will ever happen. But we must remember that Jesus is not "out there" somewhere. No, actually, Jesus is everywhere. He is omnipresent. So actually, while we were praying, He was standing beside us, listening to our request as if my brother or father was standing there. Three of us weren't standing there praying. There were four of us. Kind of like three Hebrew children in the fire with Jesus standing there next to them. But unlike the three Hebrew children, there were three visible participants and one invisible yet vitally important participant. Prayer is not a one-way street of communication. It's a two-way conversation. And yet, while we were praying, He was also over by that little girl directing her steps to find a set of keys at the exact same time we were asking Him for help. We often think satan is everywhere at once, but he is not. Only Jesus holds that ability to be at all places at one time. And as a result, praying to Him is not like the pony express. Certainly not in the way of Him hearing. Oh, it may take a long time for an answer, but He hears immediately because He is right next to you as you pray. Which leads to my second thought.

The Bible says to trust in the Lord with all your heart and lean not on your own understanding. In all your ways, *acknowledge* Him, and He will direct your paths. Because of what I stated in my last point, and oftentimes just lack of belief that God cares, we fail to acknowledge Him in the basic day-to-day things, small problems, or even silly desires we may have. I am not sure at times whether I am more amazed that God created the stars by speaking them into existence or that He actually hears my prayers and oftentimes answers my silly little requests. He's an enormous God. Creating stars seems more like what a giant God does. But speaking to me? Answering my small prayers? Blessing me with vain things that mean nothing of significance, except that He delights in giving things to his children and enjoys when we find pleasure in His blessings. We are created for His pleasure, and when we find pleasure in His blessings, that brings Him pleasure! Think about that one for a minute!

Just a small word of encouragement. Next time you set out to do something, or need something, or even want something of pure earthly enjoyment, acknowledge God in it. Ask him to direct your steps, to lead you on the path He wants you to go. His path is *always* the right path, and there is much more fulfillment at the end of every one of His paths than at the end of our paths. Sure, definitely ask for the big things, the important things! Again, He is a big God, and He can definitely do what you need Him to do. But don't forget the small things. He cares about those, too. Not so much because He cares about the lost keys or the small material enjoyment or activity you may want to enjoy, but rather He cares about the owner of the lost keys and the child that asks to enjoy a little bit of heavenly blessing on earth. You might just be surprised at how fast the God who is standing next to you listening to you pray answers your request simply because you acknowledged Him in *all* your ways. By the way, I did score a goal, and our team won... just saying!

WATCH OUT FOR SUBTLETY AND DECEPTION

This past Saturday, I watched a video on YouTube of a Canadian pastor being pulled over by a rather large entourage of police cars where they arrested him, handcuffed him, and literally carried him to a police escort. It was quite a scene on the highway. His crime—he dared to hold a service and preach.

Earlier in the evening on Saturday, I stood at the edge of the St. Lawrence River in the "free" country of America and could see neighboring Canada. Less than two miles away, a country we would have said was reasonably close to us when it comes to freedom is now arresting pastors because they exercise the religious liberty they have had. How does this even happen?

Exactly a week earlier, I was driving to New York, through the states, of course, and once I entered New York, I stopped to get gas. As I put the pump in the tank and pulled the lever, I realized that there is no pin to keep the pump running for you as you throw out garbage or just sit and wait. I remember back in the early 2000s, when I was driving every weekend to New York to visit my eventual bride, they had outlawed that. Oh, well, Not a big deal. I used the gas cap to hold it. I filled up my truck and finished my trip. A few days later, I stopped by a gas station to get some food, and when I paid, I asked the lady for a bag to carry all my stuff. She told me she was not legally allowed to give me a plastic bag for me to put my items in. There was one exception to that law, but apparently, my five items didn't qualify. Oh, well, I just grabbed my food and walked out to the truck.

A year ago, when Covid hit, basically every state shut down, the world shut down, and we were almost immediately forced to wear masks.

Remember the fourteen days to flatten the curve? Well, here we are over a year later, and most states are still requiring a mask. Now I see people driving in their cars, alone, with masks on. I see people step out of their car at a store and immediately put on their masks 150 feet from the entry door when they are required to put them on. What has happened? After a certain amount of time, most people have said, "Oh, well," and complied. And then, of course, you attach a "medical reason" and make people look like they are unloving and uncaring for their neighbor if they don't wear one, and walla, people are so quick to accept it. I certainly wish these politicians would have as much concern for the helpless unborn children as they claim to have for everyone else.

How could Canada get to a point where they could arrest a pastor when they have freedom of religion? Well, the same way New York is getting there, and many other states as well, and ultimately our country as a whole. They slowly took away our little freedoms, and because they were minor inconveniences, we just said, "Oh, well." Until now, if I understand correctly, in New York, you do not have the choice of whether you will vaccinate your children or not. Now it's a crime not to vaccinate in New York. I was told even the Amish don't have that freedom of choice anymore. For *all* of us, it was so easy to say, "Oh well," and adjust than to stand up and say you will not do that at any cost. It's too inconvenient to our lives to say, "Not going to happen." But see what, in fact, has happened? The liberal agenda has taken over our country piece by piece. It was slow. It was methodical, but they did it. The whole time we were trying to compromise, they never gave up an inch. We would win on one front and take a break. They would lose and immediately go after something else. We won battles here and there, but while we, and by *we* I mean conservatives and Christians, were winning battles, they were winning the war.

I have said enough about what has happened but what has happened in our country is really not the biggest threat to us as individuals. The biggest threat to us as individuals is us doing the same thing in our own personal lives. See, we have an adversary called the devil, and the Bible says he comes only to kill, steal, and destroy. There is zero good intention in him. He does not have a single good bone in his body. He's vile, he's evil, and the more people's lives he destroys, the happier he is. But see, he doesn't lay all his cards on the table for all to see. He comes in through deception, and he begins to take your peace, by piece. The Bible says that satan schemes against us. He is watching us and plotting how he will attack us. What are our strong points? Leave those alone for now. He goes for the weak points and begins to chip away at them, and eventually, in our weakness, even our strong spots will become weak, and then he has us. Certainly, this can happen in addiction. Very few people, whether pornography or drugs or anything else, just jump in both feet. It's the lure of each step of pleasure that eventually finds someone in chains unable to get free. Satan's promise of freedom *always* leads to bondage. But notice there is pleasure in it for a season. And it's that pleasure that lures us back time and again, until what we find is the door on the front side that looked so appealing and is so easy to open, is black and dirty on the backside with no handle to get out.

Remember what happened in 1776? Britain just outright decided they were going to regulate our nation. And look what happened. It was obvious what they were trying to do, and our country kicked their backside and kicked them out. Now, look at our country and the insane amount of taxes we have. Worse than probably what Britain was expecting. It was done over time and through subtlety.

Satan is no different. He doesn't mind taking his sweet time with you, as long as he gets you to where he wants you to be, slowly giving up your freedoms because they seem small, and it's more inconvenient to fight until one day you realize you are no longer free at all.

What has happened in our country and now in Canada has made me think about my own life and what areas I have allowed things to slip in, that if I don't shore up boundaries or take back the liberty in Christ that I have, that eventually I will be enslaved by my own choices. America is lost.

Sorry to say, I mourn daily over that fact, but it's too far gone. There is no redeeming America in the state it's in. What we have seen in Canada is right around the corner. But as individuals, we are not too far gone as long as we begin and continue to fight back against the schemes of the enemy.

The Bible says we are not to be ignorant of his devices. Why? Because if we are, he will slowly, methodically, and deceptively take away the God-given freedoms we have, and the end result is always destructive to one's soul. It's the way of death.

GOD IS THE MASTER ARCHER

Shot my bow tonight as bad as I can remember. Maybe not the worst ever but just so inconsistent. In my defense, it was at night down my driveway at thirty yards, but still. I can shoot way better. I definitely need to shoot some more before I enter the woods.

Sometimes that's how I feel with life like I've totally missed it. Hoping for the bull's eye. It seems like I'm way off target. But then I remember I'm not the one shooting the bow. The Lord never misses when He shoots the arrow. I don't need to be concerned about the target, just about being a straight-ready arrow. If I have not been released yet toward the mark, I must not be ready, or it's just not my time. Jesus silently waited for eighteen years, knowing what He was called to do. But when the Master Archer decides I'm ready to be released, I know He'll hit where He's aiming. So I'll just patiently wait here in His quiver!

If the Lord is not your archer... You have zero chance of hitting the mark for which you were born to hit. Just a thought for those of you who may read this and don't know Christ.

HE WILL FIX THE BLEMISHES

I was purging some files and came across these two pictures. Years ago, can't remember how many now, we removed an unwanted window for a client of the company I was working for, primarily as a paint supervisor. We ordered bricks that were supposed to be a dead-on match of the existing brick of the house. Of course, they weren't even close, as you can tell. The client was out of town, and we had to pull a rabbit out of the hat or lose some serious money replacing all the bricks we just had installed. It was time for the artist brushes to come out. This was not the time for production but rather precision. After working with various paints, tinting my own colors, and 200 trips... it seemed... up and down the ladder to look at the overview of the side of the house and how the paint was blending with the existing brick... walla, we were satisfied with the end result. To this day, I don't believe the client ever knew what we had to do to fix that brick! I haven't driven by that house in years. I wonder how it still looks.

It reminds me of the finger of God at work in our lives. Man, we sure can botch things up, can't we? Sometimes I honestly feel like God only works through my failures and never through anything good I have done. Right and wrong are the only two options. There should be a 50/50 chance of getting it right, don't you think? But instead, it "seems" to me the percentages are highly favoring the wrong side for me. It appears Paul was as much aware of this as I often am about myself. But Paul thankfully penned the rhetorical question, "Oh, wretched man that I am! Who shall deliver me from this body of death"? Thankfully, he didn't hesitate to mention the remedy! I thank God through Jesus Christ my Lord! Just like that day, I had to fix a messed-up side of brick on that house. The Real Artist who paints fresh, original horizons and sunsets every morning and evening takes out his brushes and begins to fix the blemishes and messes we make of ourselves. The sad part often is we think we can fix things better than God. I am convinced many, if not most, of my mistakes, would have been resolved much faster by the loving Master Painter if I had just gotten out of the way.

Maybe you have some glaring blemishes in your life that you feel they are taking too long to be rectified. May I suggest you may want to put your crusty stiff bristled paint brush down and let the Master painter use his artistry to fix... and cover... your failures?

Maybe it's taking long because it was a big blemish. Maybe years have gone by, and you're still reaping the results of really poor choices. As the old artist said when fixing Woody in *Toy Story 2*, "You can't rush art." Perfection takes time. It always took much longer to remodel a home than it did to build a new one. And when God fixes something in our lives, He does it right every time! And just like that house, one brick at a time began to disappear into the existing brick until, eventually, they all disappeared.

So, don't lose heart! The Master Painter is carefully and meticulously fixing the blotches in our lives. And however painful it may appear to be at the moment, we will be eternally grateful when we see the end result. Philippians 1:6, the promise to the Philippian church applies to us as well, "Being confident of this that He who began a good work in you will carry it on to completion until the day of Christ Jesus.

KEEP YOUR MIND AND
EYES ON JESUS

How often is it that we hear the whisper of God's voice when we least expect it? Was this experience one of those times for me? I certainly don't have some hotline to heaven, but at times a thought will come, or something will happen that will make you pause and wonder. Maybe it's what you needed for that particular time in the day. This experience that I am about to share with you was one of those times for me. Perhaps as you read, you will think little of me as I open my heart with written words and expose some of my fears. And that's fine. I am most comfortable in that position because I know anything of value that may come was not because of me but rather in spite of me.

I stopped in on a bathroom remodel that the company I work for had been doing. It was about wrapped up and, after the plumbers installed the plumbing fixtures, they left boxes all over the place. One of the fine workers I have the privilege of working with did a thorough clean-up and left the boxes organized in the bathroom. When I got there, seeing no reason to leave the boxes, I rolled up the tonneau cover of my truck and loaded the empty boxes in the back. I was concerned as I loaded them up, thinking I sure hope they don't fly out when the wind hits against them as I drive. But the events of work and getting to the next job soon invaded my thoughts as I finished loading the empty boxes.

I quickly got things cleaned up and jumped in my truck, and took off to the next destination. I enjoy driving as it often gives me a little alone time to think as things are quiet inside. As I left the job, my mind went to what was happening in this world, and honestly, the thoughts in my mind were not pleasant ones. Admittedly, my thoughts were causing some anxiety as I zipped down one road and twisted and turned down other ones.

I don't know if you are paying attention, but things are getting bad *really* fast. The things that are being pushed and forced on us are happening at unparalleled rates. Honestly, I am not too concerned for myself, but I have a wife and four young kids. My mind began to nearly panic. How will I take care of them? What would I do if this happened or that happened? How would I protect them under these circumstances? What happens if I can't get food for them as a result of taking a stand for my faith and not allowing the government to dictate my life? I love my kids. I mean, I *really love* them! And the thought of me not being able to protect or take care of them is more than I can bear! And, and, and... I had driven about five miles or so, and for the first time, I looked out the back window, and I saw this cardboard box that was folded and stuffed in another larger box fluttering like crazy in the breeze! I immediately slowed down and began to worry that it was going to fly out. *Immediately,* the thought came to me, *As long as you kept your eyes facing ahead on the road where it was supposed to be, you had no concern for that box flying out the back. But the moment you saw it, you became concerned.* The box was always fluttering in the wind, but I only started to worry when my eyes left the road ahead of me to look back. Needless to say, I never checked for that box again until I reached the dumpster another fifteen miles away. Guess what, it was still there.

I believe there is a story in the Bible much more dramatic than mine that reminds us far more vividly of where our attention should be. It's a main story in children's books. It's the story of Peter walking on the water, actually Jesus walking on water, and Peter bravely attempting to walk to Jesus. Terrible storm, Disciples frightened, Jesus comes walking up (I *love* how it says, "And he would have passed by them"... Like, "Hey, fellas, see you on the other side") and Peter says, "Lord, if it's You, bid me come" and Jesus says, "Come." Peter gets out and begins to walk on the water toward Jesus. He must have gotten a decent distance away from the boat because when he started to sink, he could have just grabbed onto the boat. But instead, he cries out to Jesus as he begins to sink. Peter's only mistake was that his eyes wandered from the face and hands of Jesus to the waves around him. His attention to Jesus was interrupted by the surrounding circumstances. The waves were real. The peril the disciples were in was real. But so was Jesus. And the moment Peter took his eyes off the answer and began to focus on the problem, he began to sink.

No doubt things are getting very bad in this world, at an incredible rate of speed! But it's important to remember that even in the midst of the greatest turmoil the world will ever see that John explains, he mentions the throne having a sea of glass in front of it. Not a ripple! Not a single pebble of anxiety or fear, or uncertainty can ripple the sea of glass that is before the Father's throne. Because He's completely in charge!

Your personal world might be in that position where the waves of life are rocking your boat. There are so many things that can buffet us in this world. And perhaps you find yourself with that same anxious feeling. The truth of the word of God applies as much to you. Keep your focus on Jesus. Look to Him for answers. Don't concentrate on the waves around you or the fluttering cardboard box in the back of the truck bed. Keep your focus. Don't allow distractions to cause you to turn your head to the right or left.

Isaiah 26:3 so clearly states the issue I had this day. "You will keep in perfect peace those whose minds are steadfast because they trust in you." My problem was, and so often is, that my eyes are not focused on the right thing. I am concentrating on the fluttering cardboard boxes of life instead of keeping my eyes on "The Way" in front of me! But for me, and for you, the only way to keep peace in storms is to keep my attention on the One who walks about the waves and cuts through the fierce wind as if it does not exist.

That little cardboard incident was enough for me on that day to realign my perspective to where it should be. Oh, I will need something else again, probably in the near future. Because the wind is real, the waves are real, the storm is getting worse, and I get easily distracted.

But peace comes to me and to those who are able to discipline their eyes to look forward amid all the noise of crashing waves. I am so thankful there is a constant Light House that is always visible through faith to anyone who will choose to focus on its beaming ray of light. Lord knows I daily need its guidance!

DESTROYING THE COUNTRY FROM THE INSIDE OUT

The date was October 22, 2018. The place was in the US courthouse in downtown Detroit. No, I was not there for criminal reasons. I was there to watch my wife become a US citizen. Technically I should have already been on the road as I had won a hunt through bizarre circumstances to a whitetail deer outfitter in Southern Ohio for that last week of October bow season, but my wife had gotten the letter from the government that on October 22nd she was going to take the oath to become officially American.

We had married back in 2002. After the ceremony in Guatemala, her native country, I had to come home alone because we didn't have the proper paperwork ready at the time, so she couldn't come back with me. Thankfully she was able to get a visitor's visa to come to the states for six months, but then she would have to leave again. Needless to say, through some serious investigation, paperwork, money, and an act of God, she never had to leave.

We made sure we did everything legally, and she got her green card, and for sixteen years, she lived here as a legal alien. In some ways, she was able to experience most of the benefits our country had to offer, but not entirely. It came the time for her ten-year green card to be renewed, and we both agreed that she should become a citizen. She certainly was excited, and so was I. So we applied for her citizenship, we paid like 725 dollars or something like that, and then we waited. Finally, she received a notice that she would have to come in for a test, and they gave her a booklet to study for the test she was going to have to take. She doesn't like to do anything mediocre, and this was no exception. She studied as hard as she could. She wanted to do everything right to become a citizen. Not just barely squeak in.

Finally, that day came, and we headed to an immigration building where we sat in this massive lobby waiting for her to be called to take her oral test. After some time, they called her name, and I watched her walk behind the immigration officer, who stopped to let her walk through the massive door, which he then closed. Honestly, I was never concerned because I knew she had done her homework, and she had already overcome a ton of obstacles just by moving away from home at nineteen. She, of course, aced the test. Got every question right, and then the officer told her that she would get a letter in the mail as to when she would go to the courthouse and take the oath of citizenship.

Well, there we were at the courthouse on October 22nd. I had postponed my trip for one day so we could go to her appointment. As we walked into the courthouse and went through the security, they led us into a courtroom where there were around 150 people, I would guess of all different races and nationalities representing around seventy-five different countries with their wives or husbands or families waiting to watch their family member become a citizen. It was pretty interesting to watch people. There was a silent excitement in the air. As we sat there with our four kids, you could feel the anticipation as everyone waited for the judge to come and do whatever it was a judge did at one of these ceremonies.

Finally, after what seemed forever, and not because I had to leave for Ohio, but rather because of the anticipation of the event, the judge walked in, we all stood to honor him, and I wondered in my mind what this was going to look like.

He started off by mentioning that his parents were immigrants that came to America in the early 1900s, and he showed pictures on a projector screen of the boat. Then he began to paint the most beautiful picture with words of what America was about. A place of opportunity, a place of freedom, a place of freedom to serve your own good, a place to pursue your dream, and the list went on and on. By the time he was done, I couldn't have felt more proud to be an American. He talked with such grace and yet conviction as to what every new citizen could be or pursue as their dream. His perspective was of what I would wish every American or person who lives in America would think of this country.

After he had given such a touching speech, he had all the people who were becoming citizens stand and raise their right hand and repeat the oath after him. Honestly, it brings tears to my eyes, thinking of how the myriad of voices and accents from all over the world repeated the oath swearing their allegiance to America. And every person there was thankful for the opportunity to become an American citizen. It was a time of rejoicing and celebration. We clapped when they were finished, and the judge kindly took a picture with each person or family that became a citizen. We took some pictures for a few married couples, and I exchanged numbers so I could send them the pictures. It was what coming to this country and becoming American was supposed to be.

I don't think there has ever been a time in my life when I was more proud of the country I lived in. Open arms to those who wanted a better life in America. They came legally. They paid their time and paid their dues because, to them, it was worth it. They saw something in our country that made them want to leave their own and become a citizen here.

I was proud of our country then, and I am proud of our country now! Oh, I know we have issues, major issues that need to be addressed. But as long as this earth exists in its present state, there will always be issues with our country and every country. Because people make up a country. But in our country, we have always recognized that we hold these truths to be self-evident and that all men are created by the... you... you... you know the thing! Sorry, I just couldn't resist.

The problem with our country is not having issues, even major issues that need to be addressed. The problem with our country is there are those in it, from the normal citizen to the tainted evil professor all the way up to our highest office, who are trying to destroy our country from within. They are not Americans. They are not trying to solve the problems we have. They are trying to capitalize on the problems we have to promote an agenda that is not and has never been American. They cry racism while they themselves are promoting it. They cry life is precious while they themselves are destroying lives upward of sixty million murdered/aborted babies. They cry for equal rights for everyone while they do everything in their power to keep minorities dependent on them so they can get their votes. They cry for equal rights, and yet they will take one's rights away in a moment if it does not line up with their plans. Freedom of speech is fine until it goes against their agenda. They can spew out the most vicious things about anyone they choose, but don't attack them, or you are bigoted and racist and evil. They cry foul on the second amendment the whole time, promoting violence in their own controlled inner cities. They give billions of dollars away to other nations while withholding it from those in need in our own country, their allegiance is to other countries, not our beloved America.

See, we look at their inconsistencies, and we say how hypocritical and how sad but fail to realize they don't care. They don't care about morality. They don't care about the majority. They don't care about consistency. What they care about is controlling and transforming our nation into a place that fits their evil agenda. Lying and stealing from its own people is just a means to get them to their ultimate destination where they control, and we become a global nation.

America is a good nation founded by good people. And please don't say, oh, they did some bad things. Thank you, Mr. Perfect, for your astute observation. No one is perfect. But they created a good country that was made not for themselves but for the people of the country. When they did see evil in it, they were willing to fight to the death to purge it from the enslavement of other men and women created in the image of God. Fathers, husbands, and sons are willing to die to free someone they never met. An estimated 620,000 dead in the line of duty. Roughly two percent of the population, correcting an egregious wrong. The problem isn't America as a nation. The problem is those inside it that want to sabotage it for their own evil agenda.

What has happened to the land that I love? We are being taken over from the inside out. I can guarantee you that not one of those people who became American citizens that day came because they wanted to be ruled over and lose freedoms, and forced to live and accept certain things that were not part of their world or moral view. No, their dream was to experience life, liberty, and the pursuit of happiness.

I am afraid that America being forced upon us today will remain just that for most in the near future... a dream. Certainly, at the moment, we are living in a nightmare as we watch the crumbling of the world's greatest nation to ever exist at the hands of a minority of people through the means of politics and "social justice" deceit.

America, I will always love you. I will always value and appreciate the country you were, the men you created that served our nation to the death as well as those who fought on foreign soil to keep us free, the good you have done in the world, and the freedoms you gave every legal citizen who came to this great nation. You won't be around forever. One day soon, you will be brought down. But while you existed, you made the world a better place! You have done far more good to the world than every other country combined. The world is forever indebted to your existence, as am I!

LEARN FROM MISTAKES

Years ago, I was helping my cousin build a playhouse for his children, oh, probably seventeen or eighteen years ago. It was a pretty detailed play set and took us the entire day and well into the night. We resorted to one person holding the flashlight and the other doing the manual labor, which by now was pretty much just attaching the finishing touches with bolts, nuts, and washers. It was approximately 11 p.m., and we only had about twenty minutes more to go. I slipped a bolt through the hole about stomach to chest high and started to put the washer on, and somehow it slipped out of my hand off the end of the bolt and onto the ground. My cousin shined the light on the ground in the general area, and I bent down to pick it up, except I spent the next five minutes looking for a stupid little washer about the size of a penny but black. I could not for the life of me find where in the world that washer had fallen. Seriously, how hard can it be to find a black washer in the grass? I had looked very hard. It's not going to bounce, and it could only be in about a twelve-inches circle. This was ridiculous! My cousin had all but given up and was ready to move on when suddenly I had an idea. I told him to hand me the last washer we had for the last bolt and told him to shine his light on the ground. Once he did that, I took that last washer, slowly placed it on the bolt, and did my best to mimic what happened when the other one had fallen off. As I slipped it on, then allowed it to fall off, it fell to the ground and made the unmistakable sound of metal hitting metal. We saw where that one landed, and I reached down and grabbed both washers. He told me to quiet down because it was late. But my silly scheme of recreating my first goof-up worked to perfection! I kind of get excited thinking about it as I am writing this.

I am often amazed how people make the same mistakes over and over again and never seem to stop and pay attention to what happened the first time to try and avoid it. In this particular instance, I purposefully tried to recreate the scenario to get the same result, and it worked. Unfortunately, so often, we make a mistake and never stop to consider why it happened. And as a result, they keep stumbling over the same bumps in the road they always have.

I know this one guy that has goofed up tons of times in the exact same way over the course of his life. And every time he would mess up, he would tell himself, *I will never do that again! This is the last time,* only to do it all over again. Finally, he said to himself one day, *Philip, if you don't learn from your mistakes and change your behavior, it doesn't matter how many times you promise to never do it again, you will.* Yep, that person is me! But I bet I'm not alone in that scenario, which in a weird sort of way brings me a little comfort.

Have you ever repeatedly done something that drives you nuts after you have done it, but it's only a matter of time until you head back to that same old well? Most of the time, that happens in cases of addiction, things like pornography, terrible eating habits, alcoholism, or smoking. It can often happen in other areas of weakness like being late for work, yelling at the kids or wife or husband, or having that loose tongue of slander or gossip. There are so many ways to repeat mistakes. After all, we are human, and to be human is to fail.

Sadly for most if not all of us, with me being the chief example, we could avoid the same traps we so often fall into if we just take a careful examination of how we got there in the first place. Believe me; I know how it goes. Goof up, feel guilty, make it right, promise to never do it again and forget about it and move on... until the next time. The thing that was missing in that list was to do a careful examination of how you got into that spot in the first place and come up with an intentional plan to avoid the same pitfall the next time. I know, I said that dirty word "intentional." Like my cousin that night, we are so quick to just move on without figuring out what went wrong and how to avoid it. Let's face it. We work hard. We are busy. Our minds are on a million things. We don't have time to think about it. Well, if you don't and I don't, we might as well start the crazy cycle again because it's only a matter of time before we fall into the same trap again.

No battle is ever won, no addiction is ever broken, and no bad life habit ever beat without a good intentional plan. Yes, we can spend our whole life working on one issue after another. So let's start with one. What is the one thing you really want to beat? Go after that one. Start there. Make a plan. Get help. Team up with someone. Let go of the excuses and don't let repeated failure convince you can't change. You and I are only one intentional plan away from making it happen! As Larry, the cable guy, so profoundly put it, "Get 'er done!"

KEEP LOOKING FOR THAT CITY— DON'T GET DISTRACTED

The year was 1999. The time was right after deer season. I was the quintessential weekend warrior. Even though I was single, that was about all I could afford at the time. Not to mention my hunting spot was an hour and forty-five minutes away. I tried a couple of evening hunts, and let's just say it didn't seem quite worth it, especially hunting public land in the heavily hunted county of Tuscola, Michigan, outside of a little town called Cass City, at the end of a street called Crawford. I don't hunt there anymore, so I don't mind giving away my spot. I did shoot a decent eight-point my first year there in 1997, but things went downhill very fast after that. But I don't want to talk about it.

One of the cool parts about this area is that my cousins had a 120-acre field they hunted about three miles away. Behind their field was solid woods for a long way. There were tons of deer back there, and they would head to the field to feed in the evening and back into the woods in the morning. There were times they would see upwards of fifty deer, typically no big bucks, mind you but lots of deer. But it's not always about big bucks, and consequently, we made some great memories on the weekends with a bunch of us hunting public and my cousins hunting their lease. We would rent a couple of hotel rooms and all pile in them and then go to our hunting spots and convene at the hotel, share notes, grab lunch and head back out for the evening hunt. I can't tell you how much fun that was!

One day shortly after hunting season, my cousin and I went up to their property for reasons which I can't quite remember to be honest, but it doesn't really matter. The point was we had to do something at the back of the property, which was probably 1200 yards from the main road to the back. This field they hunted at the time was just nothing but weeds. I believe if I remember correctly, the government actually paid the farmer not to farm the field. I have no idea why. The only thing in the field which made it easy to walk through the grass was a beat-down spot where their truck had made a path from driving up and down it several times. All the weeds were there, just matted down.

On this particular day, he and I set out from the parking spot and made our way to the back. If you know me at all, you will know that I like to find lost things. As we were walking back, he told me that he had lost a gold screw to the sights somewhere on his bow when he had been walking out there the last time. He had searched and searched but couldn't find it. The gold piece was the size of a pea, so it was no surprise. But for me, it was game on. Naturally, we were engrossed in conversation the entire time, but my mind didn't fully forget that something gold, the size of a pea, was lost in this 120-acre field. The only information I had was what the piece was, he had lost it on the two-track, and I believe there was a few hundred-yard section in which he was pretty sure he had lost it.

We walked to the back of the property, did whatever it was we went out there to do and left to come back out. Again as we walked out, there was plenty of chatter. I know for me in life, there are several things that I never tire of talking about. Definitely, my favorite is about the ways of God! Another one is deer hunting. I have a feeling it was probably that way with him as well, and so my guess is our conversation had something to do with one of those two things.

About halfway back, as we were talking, something caught my eye, but what I saw didn't connect with my brain at that moment, and we kept walking. We probably walked another twenty yards or so, and suddenly, I realized that I had seen that little gold screw lying on the ground in the weeds. I immediately stopped and told him I had just seen his screw, to which I think he was a little bit shocked and probably in disbelief. But because it didn't register in my brain right away, I had to go back a little way and retrace my steps. Sure enough, as I retraced my steps somehow, I was able to pick out that gold screw lying beneath the weeds. My legacy (in my own mind) lived on for another day! We were both pretty pleased, to say the least, and for different reasons, to be sure. He was happy to get his gold screw back, and I felt very accomplished that I had found the "needle in the haystack."

Life is so much like our little journey that he and I took that day. Our conversation is like all the distractions we face. My cousin, being older, I am sure, was doing most of the talking, and he probably never realized that even though I was listening and talking, in the back of my brain, I was still looking for that gold screw, almost subconsciously. Think of how our lives are full of distractions to what is important to the point that if we aren't paying attention, we are going to miss the big picture of what life is really about. You may be thinking that I am referring to witnessing and spreading the gospel. As important as that is, I am not. What I am referring to is a kingdom that is coming and very possibly coming soon, which includes spreading the gospel. The Bible says of Abraham in Hebrews 11:10 that by faith, Abraham was looking forward to the city with foundations, whose architect and builder is God. Abraham's story is quite remarkable and really quite adventuresome, whether he wanted it to be or not. But regardless of conquering kings and saving his nephew, dealing with Hagar the servant and his wife Sarah who he bare children for both, regardless of letting his nephew pick the best land and he got stuck with the crummy spot, and the list goes on, Abraham never forgot that this world was only a temporary place for him and that his real home was in a different kingdom with a different city and a benevolent king.

No doubt there is a tremendous amount of turmoil happening on this earth. Not to mention all the turmoil we may have in our own lives. World chaos, political chaos, possibly family chaos, work chaos, relational chaos, division in our nation, and the list goes on and on. If we don't keep our eyes lifted toward the horizon, we can and often will become overwhelmed with what is going on in our lives. We may not be able to change the chaos we are in, but we can soar above the chaos when we keep our eyes on the eternal city that is truly our final home.

No matter what happens on this earth, and should the whole world be destroyed by it turning on itself, there is a kingdom coming that all who profess the name of Christ will enter one day and enjoy its splendor... forever!

With all of life's distractions, let's not forget to keep a keen eye for that kingdom that is to come. It may appear to be as difficult to see as that little gold screw in a field of weeds. But if we allow ourselves to get too distracted, we could be like the five foolish virgins and not be ready when it does happen... And it's gonna happen.

Keep your eyes on the horizon... This troubled world is not our final home!

MY DAUGHTER'S CAR ACCIDENT

I was out of town in New York doing some painting for my brother. Watertown, NY, is where I grew up, and quite frankly, I thoroughly enjoyed my childhood. It's very much in the country, and I am not a city person by any stretch, regardless of now having lived in a Detroit suburb for over twenty-four years. Being back in my old area, instead of taking the fastest way back to my brother's house each night after work, there were a couple of nights that I took a long way home and drove past the house I grew up in. That particular night, as I drove by the house, tears welled up in my eyes as I began to relive some of the memories. I realized that part of my heart was still there, and I so desperately wanted to walk to the side door we always entered into the house and knock and see if the present owners would let me just walk the house one more time and relive my childhood and the memories I had in each room. From my perspective, it was a country boy's dream to live in that house. I didn't stop to ask, but for a couple of nights, I drove by it as I accepted that it was pretty much a past life and there was no need to go back to it.

I had started painting for my brother on Sunday and by Friday at 5 p.m. I had finished our goal and had packed up most of my things with the idea that I would work for him one more day on Saturday and then leave at 4 p.m. and return home to my family. That particular night, not only did I take the long way back to his house, I decided I was going to just drive all the back roads I used to bike on, and many people from our old church lived or once lived on. I was in no hurry. I was really enjoying just slowly driving down each country road, remembering the old one-armed guy that went to our church. How he lost his arm and survived is a whole story in and of itself. But he had 400 acres he let me hunt, and over the course of several years, we became reasonable friends, even with such an age gap. I drove past the one family's house that was on one side of the road and barn on the other. We often went there as kids and would shoot frogs down at the creek behind the barn in the summer and play hide and seek at night in the barn in the winter. Farther down that road, there used to be a barn we called the Red Barn (how original), where we often would go rabbit hunting in the winter. As I was driving down the different country roads, even the memory of the lay of the roads came back to me. I would remember the bump here, or the little hill, where as you sped down it, your stomach tingled almost like going down a hill on a roller coaster. Right after that little dip, you come up the other side, and there is a house that people from our church used to live in. I remembered that when I was a little boy, the owners at that time had a pool, and that was where I was baptized at seven years old. I was really enjoying....

Suddenly my phone rings and as I look down, I see it's my daughter calling who went to her friend's house so they could go to her friend's church later that evening. Just fifteen minutes earlier, she had told me she "really missed me." Somewhat confused, I interrupt my reminiscing and answer the phone. I can barely hear her, but something doesn't sound right, and then we get cut off. Right away, she calls me again, and this time, I can hear her very clearly as she is panicking and telling me that they had just gotten in a terrible car accident on the highway. They were driving down the highway at seventy miles per hour when another suburban hit the suburban she was riding in along with the driver and three other girls, and the driver lost control of the vehicle they were in. My daughter was in the middle row buckled, and the three girls were in the far back row not buckled. As the driver lost control, the suburban did a complete 360 on the highway, rolled backward, and slammed into the guard rail. At that moment of impact, both the back window and the side window exploded and shattered to pieces. They hit the guardrail once more and eventually roll to a stop on the road again.

My daughter, who is getting slammed around in complete shock, turns around to look at her friends, and all three of them are gone as no longer in the suburban. All three were ejected out the back window of the suburban. My daughter really starts to panic as she tells the driver that his daughter and two nieces are not in the back. The anxiety he begins to feel is horrific, and my daughter, who is banged up on her knee and arm, immediately calls 911. She ends up handing the phone to the driver, and once they are off, she immediately calls me.

By then, she had a reasonable idea of what happened and the condition of the other three. When she called me the second time, her first words were, "We got in a terrible accident, but we are all fine!" Then proceeded to tell me that three of the girls were ejected from the vehicle, and one of them landed on the other side of the guard rail... Without going into the rest of our conversation I had with her, and subsequent conversations, including with an officer who was at the scene, here is what appeared to happen

They are headed down the main highway at seventy miles per hour. They get sideswiped by another suburban crossing lanes without apparently realizing they are beside the woman driver, and their suburban spins out of control. The moment they hit the guardrail, the back window and side window immediately smashed, the back seat the three girls were sitting in broke at impact, and the first girl flew out the back over the guardrail, and the other two, somehow, some way, both went out the back as well and landed on the pavement. The truck rolls to a stop, and my daughter informs the driver his daughter and two nieces are gone. He gets out and immediately goes to see what horror he is going to find. The girl that flew over the guardrail is standing up, looking for her sister. She finds her, and they both go over to the daughter, who is laying on the ground because she had hit her head, but she was wide awake. A nurse happened to be driving to the hospital for the night shift that they ended up going to, and she had bandages and pads to help stop the bleeding on the girl's legs from getting cut as they flew through the window opening with broken glass. All four of the girls were in dresses because they were headed to church.

There is even more to that whole scene, but the paramedics showed up and took all 4 of them in separate ambulances to the same hospital.

All four had X-rays and not a single broken bone in their bodies. One had twenty-eight stitches. One had a concussion. The other had some stitches as well, and my daughter had a bruised knee and bruised arm with several bruises on other parts of her body. Other than that, they were fine. The driver had bruises and cuts as well but was too worried about the four girls, so the doctors never checked him out. Last I heard, he was still alive... a little humor there. I immediately called my wife and told her to get to the hospital, and she and my oldest daughter left their shopping and headed to the hospital. When the police officer showed up, he thought my wife was the mom of the four girls, and he said to her, "Here are some of the belongings we cleaned up off the road." There were a few things like a purse and, I think, a phone, and he handed her three Bibles and said to her, "Someone was watching out for those girls tonight. None of them should be alive. That just doesn't happen!" The nurse in the room agreed, and he repeated it one more time to my wife. The doctor echoed the same thing when he talked to my wife and said that the young lady sitting in the middle seat, if she hadn't had her seat belt on, would have most certainly gotten it worse than any of them. A few weeks later, when I talked to the officer that gave my wife the Bibles, he reiterated the same thing to me he had told her. He told me it was a miracle and that in sixty percent of accidents where someone is ejected out of a vehicle, the person loses their life. But that day, three girls who were ejected out of the vehicle and my daughter with her seat belt on in the vehicle, bruised and battered, walked out of the hospital on their own feet!

Just the night before this happened, my nephew and I were talking, and he asked me, "Why don't we see many miracles?" My answer to him was because, in America, we have an answer for everything. If we are in financial trouble, we go get a loan. If we have a health issue, we go to the doctor. If it's a serious health issue, we have health insurance. I said, "We have our own solutions to problems. But in other third-world countries where they don't have the ability to solve all of their problems, many have to turn to God, and He often takes care of them with miracles. Miracles in other parts of the world are not as rare as they are here." But less than twenty-four hours later, a suburban was driving down the highway and lost complete control and was at the mercy of whatever was going to happen. They had no control, they had no answer, no quick fix, so Jesus stepped in. He didn't stop the accident from happening, but He somehow some way took a life-altering accident with three young teenage girls in dresses, being ejected out a back window (must have been single file) and a fourth girl (my daughter), who didn't even remember being buckled in but was, and He kept them safe enough that with only cuts and bruises and several lessons to be learned, they walked out of the hospital that very night.

Some would say those girls are the luckiest girls in the world. As if somehow four girls just happened to survive a crash like that. This was not one girl, or two girls, or three girls... It was four girls, all safe and alive. It's not luck. It's called a miracle! And the reason it is a miracle is that there is a God who does miracles at times and in ways of His choosing. And that night, He decided that even though the wreck warranted certainly the death of three little girls flying out of a window on a highway after slamming into a guardrail, He was not going to allow it because it was not their time.

Life is short, and at times, it changes in a second. I was enjoying calling to memory all the experiences I had as a kid, and out of the blue, my daughter called me in a panic. Had something been more wrong and my daughter had lost her life, I can't tell you how important her last text to me would have been, "I really miss you." That would have become the most important text in my life. I had purposed that week that while I was gone, I would make sure through communication of phone calls or texts or audio texts that they would know how much I loved them. Just in case... something like that was to happen to me. Because once it's done, it's done. We all have loved ones. Don't hesitate to tell them you love them. Don't wait to give them a hug. Don't wait to make that one offense right. I mentioned it to my other daughter, who was waiting at the hospital as well. I told her all those arguments don't seem to matter now, do they?" She agreed. It's not worth it. Life is often much shorter than we anticipate, and if we hesitate to do or say the things we know we should and possibly even want to, we may regret it for the rest of our lives. This was one of those times when things could have been very different. But I know I had done the best I could while I was away to let her know how much I loved her and missed her. Not saying I love you or showing that act of kindness or forgiveness could become the biggest thing we regret... if we just don't do it.

DON'T LET IT SLIP ANOTHER DAY!

P.S. I drove through the night and got home at 6 a.m. the following morning. Those five-hour energy drinks really do work!

LOST KEY—CONFESS YOUR SINS THAT YOU MAY BE HEALED

Do you hate losing stuff? I do. How many of us actually enjoy looking for things that are lost? I bet not very many, and this is probably where I would end up being in the minority. I actually enjoy looking for things that are hard to find. Maybe it's because I always lose or misplace things. That desire has definitely lessened some over the years but not entirely. I have quite a list of unusual finds and lessons I learned from them in the process.

One such time had to do with a client's key that I was entrusted with while they were away on vacation. This particular key was wrapped with a Detroit Pistons logo and was the main key to their house. We were working on their house while they were away as well as working on many other houses at the same time. I was working in between two jobs that were about 4 miles apart and traveling back and forth sometimes, multiple times a day.

One particular day while I was making rounds, I foolishly set the key on the back bumper while I was getting something out of the back of the truck. I forgot about it, and after I got what I needed, I jumped into my truck and sped off. I made a couple of specific stops, one being the bank before I got to the job, only to realize I didn't have the key and had no idea where it was. This was on a Friday. For the next hour or two, I retraced my steps four or five times. I drove from the job to the bank, to my other stop, and back to the job again. I walked all around where I had parked and nothing. I was pretty frustrated and felt like an idiot... Hmmm. I wonder why? If the shoe fits... On Monday, I did the same thing a couple of times and still couldn't find the key. I had now spent several hours looking for that key and drove the path I had driven a good half dozen times and nothing, naturally. I had driven four miles one way, and the possibility of a key bouncing off and falling into the weeds as it bounced off the road was pretty good.

I eventually told my boss what happened, and he said, "Well, we are going to have to tell the clients and look like complete idiots." I had pretty much resorted to the fact that he was correct, and I was going to have to eat humble pie.

But as I was contemplating how I was going to do that and break the news, I prayed one more time that the Lord would help me find that key, and at that very moment, I felt a still small voice say to me, "You're not going to find that key unless you make it right." Make what right, you ask? Well, I had lied to my boss about something the week prior, non-work related, and that thought came back to haunt me that I needed to correct it. I needed to call him up and let him know. So now I am convicted of a lie I had told, and I can't find the key I had lost. What was I supposed to do? Well, thankfully, under the circumstances of already having had to humble myself to tell my boss about the key, I continued down the humiliating road and called my boss back, told him what I had done, how I had lied, and asked that he would forgive me. As always, he was very gracious, and that at least got one thing off my mind. But I still had a lost key. Immediately after I confessed to him, I decided to look one more time and make the round I had made a half dozen times already. I hopped in my truck and very carefully began to inspect the side of the road for that key. I drove all the way to the bank, and nothing. I decided I would just go back to the job, and as I pulled out and started turning left. I just happened to look to my right on the ground, and there, laying on the side of the road, at the edge of the driveway, was that key! It had been laying there the entire weekend. To say I was relieved is an understatement! I had driven that crazy route six times. How in the world did I happen to see it the seventh time?

I learned several things in this situation that have helped me when it comes to life's frustrations. The first is that God doesn't waste opportunities, even our mistakes. And oftentimes, what seems like a natural problem there is an eternal lesson. So often, we are focused on the problem at hand that we forget there might be a much bigger reason for this problem. Kind of like Job, right? He had no idea what was going on. All he could see was his natural circumstance, but when God was done with him, he was twice the man he was before, with a much clearer picture of the sovereignty of God. I am not suggesting that for every single thing that happens to us, we need to find out what the spiritual lesson is. But there are times when things happen to us that are just not normal. They are much bigger than just getting a sliver in the finger. Sometimes it's just good to pause for a second and contemplate what is going on and why? You may realize that the answer is much deeper than just the visible issue you are dealing with at the moment. And there just might be a lesson that you can make part of your life to help you grow as a person, as a Christian.

Another thing I learned in this situation is that sometimes it's best to stop and listen. I love what Dr. Grant Woods, a biologist, says at the end of every one of his YouTube videos, "Get out and enjoy creation, but most importantly, take time to listen to what the Creator is saying to you." There are a lot of people out there that believe that God doesn't speak anymore. Somehow, because the Bible was finished, His relationship with humanity is only limited to that book. I don't believe the Bible teaches that, and it certainly hasn't been my experience. I certainly don't have an open phone line to heaven, not by any stretch. But, there have been distinct times in my life when I was thankfully sensitive enough to hear Him speak to me, or maybe it was just that He opened my deaf ears to hear both out of warning and kindness like this particular time. I firmly believe the Lord wants to have a personal relationship with His creation, and that includes, at times of His choosing, Him speaking to us. That is, if we are listening. This situation was one more example and lesson for me to learn when the Lord is speaking, in this case, with an ultimatum. Repent for lying, or you won't find the key. And I am hundred percent convinced had I not humbled myself, I would not have found that key.

Maybe something is happening in your life that, from a natural perspective, cannot be explained. Maybe it's time to stop and listen. One of the things I have learned is that you don't have to fabricate the voice of the Lord. Just listen, and you will know because your faith that He does speak *is* the listening. Sometimes even in listening, He may not speak, but I think you and I will find that most of the time, the problem is not that He doesn't want to speak to us. It's that we aren't taking the time to listen. I am thankful that through my failure, I was broken enough to listen that day. I had to humble myself to my boss and repent to him. But it still was better than having to humble myself to a client and look like an idiot. I think that's called the justice and mercy of God working in tandem with each other, as they so often do.

A life lesson for me, all from one mishap with a silly little key.

ACCEPT HELP... IF YOU WANT TO GET OUT OF THE RUT

The year was 1996. The month was early November. I was about a mile back into the woods, slowly sneaking my way down a ravine to a creek bottom. About twenty feet down the side, I caught movement to my left at the bottom. I froze behind the tree and slowly raised my rifle to look through my scope and see what the deer was. Much to my excitement, it had five points, and with only a couple bucks to my name, this one was about to find out what happens when you walk by a trigger-happy teenager who had a buck tag in his pocket!

For those who haven't hunted, it's hard to explain the rush of adrenaline and the incredible beating of the heart at the moment you are about to squeeze the trigger on a wild animal, for me, a whitetail buck! I have had some exciting times in my life with sports and other competitions, but nothing comes close to that adrenaline rush of hunting.

Completely oblivious to me, the buck walked along the creek, browsing on what food it could find. I impatiently waited until he finally entered the opening, where I had a clear shot. Being raised in the country and around guns my whole life, thank you, Dad, that buck pretty much had no chance of escaping, especially at only forty yards. I eased the trigger of my 7600 30-06 pump rifle, and at the crack of the rifle, he went down right where he had stood.

Now imagine taking that initial adrenaline rush and multiplying it by about twenty. Well, that's what happens once you successfully take a deer. The shakes are nearly uncontrollable, and the excitement is through the roof. You just beat a deer in its natural elements, and there is quite the excitement in doing that, especially as a teenager with not many deer under his belt. My day could not have gotten any better. But it was about to get a lot worse.

As I mentioned at the beginning, I was about a mile back in the woods. About 1,000 yards of that mile was field, and the rest were brush and woods. It was going to be hard enough pulling him up out of the ravine, but I thought I would get him out of there and drag him to the field and just drive my brother's four-wheel-drive pick-up truck he let me borrow to the edge of the field and load it up. I had all the time I needed, so there was no hurry. I could just take my time getting it to the field. After quite some time, I managed to get it to the edge of the field and left it there while I went back to get the truck. The whole time I was, of course, super excited and thanking God for the awesome experience of being able to harvest a buck on a beautiful day in the beautiful woods with my beautiful rifle and my beautiful brother (okay, that was weird) letting me use his beautiful truck to drive back in the beautiful field to load up my beautiful buck. Did I mention it was a beautiful buck?

All was good, good that is, until I got about halfway back in the field, and I started to feel the truck begin to sink as I was driving along the edge of the wood line. Remembering It had four-wheel drive, I stopped and popped it into four-wheel drive and proceeded to hit the gas pedal only to sink all the way up to the axles in mud. The ground seemed so firm when I was walking on it, but not when a couple thousand-pound truck was driving on it. My first thought was oh well, I'll just rock it back and forth like we do in the winter when the vehicle is stuck, but that didn't work. I rocked and rocked, and pretty soon, the rut I had created was about fifty feet long, and I was as deep as I was before. Remember how everything was beautiful, not thirty minutes before? Well, not so much anymore. Regretfully, in my immaturity, I went from such joy to using words I hadn't used in many, many years, thanks to my dad's paddle. The excitement was gone, the frustration of an awesome day going completely south was there, and my brother's truck, which was a dark midnight blue, was literally covered top to bottom with mud. I have a picture somewhere as proof. I decided to go up to the guy's property who went to our church, get some boards and try to get it out that way. I spent probably four hours or more trying to get that truck out, and nothing I did worked. I was literally helpless. I remember standing there looking at the mess I had made, tired, dirty, and frustrated.

Finally, after several hours of this insanity, I "think" it was my brother who was able to get ahold of the farmer who actually farmed the field, and he drove down with his tractor, hooked up a chain, and within twenty seconds lifted my truck out of those deep ruts, and it was over. He laughed and said to me, "Yeah, you would think that driving down the side of the field is actually the best spot, but in this field, you have to drive right down the middle." That's exactly what I did and picked up my buck and drove out with no issues from then on out. Cost twenty dollars for the farmer to get it out. That's a lot of money for a sub shop worker making minimum wage at the time, which was four thirty-five dollars per hour.

That crazy scenario, as funny as it is now, is so accurate to so many people's lives spiritually and naturally, mine included. There are things in our lives that we have dug such ruts to that no matter how hard we try and no matter how determined we think we are, and we can be determined, we are helpless at getting out of that rut! I am no stranger to ruts. If I look at my life, it feels like that beautiful field that is trashed from all the ruts in it caused by me. But I know I am not alone in that. Ruts or bad habits are so easy to create. And once we are in them, we can't get out. Oh, I made it fifty feet forward from where I originally got stuck, but I was still in the same rut that I created when I started. I just made it worse, and it was a lot longer. Many times they are created when we are young and foolish, and they carry into our later years.

My point in all this is, just like I was helpless until that farmer came along with the right equipment, experience and help, we are helpless in our ruts until we reach our hand out to someone who is not in that rut and let them help pull us out. For one, the farmer knew that field. He knew where the pitfalls were. In fact, when he pulled me out, he didn't come from straight in front or right behind. He stayed on the solid part of the field and pulled me out sideways. Sorry, Steve, for that broken bumper on the underside! There are ruts that we are in that we will never get out of without the assistance and help of a friend, a church leader, or someone who is willing to come alongside us and say, "Let me help." The Bible says we are to bear one another's burdens. That involves two people minimum. One person willing to take time out of their lives to stop and see the need of another person and is willing to walk alongside them. It's inconvenient, It's time-consuming, It's often frustrating, and there often is no kickback or visible reward. I believe that is called love. But on the other hand, if you are the one in the rut, it takes humility and a teachable spirit, and as it cost me twenty dollars, it's going to cost you as well. Mainly your pride which isn't a bad thing. I told someone recently that as fellow humans, we were never meant to walk through life alone. God put us all here to help one another. But that takes at least two people. And through those relationships, we can all be connected as we help someone get out of their rut while someone else helps us get out of ours. What a much better connection than Facebook or social media could ever be. I am quite confident for all of us that we can both immediately think of someone who is in a rut and try to help them and also our own ruts we are stuck in where we can reach out for help. I pray we all have eyes to see those in need and be willing to help them get free from their muddy, dirty ruts. But just like my brother's truck, we all can get cleaned up and then help someone else do the same.

HEAVEN'S JOYS OVERRIDES EARTH'S DISAPPOINTMENTS

Here is just a little something to think about, Specifically for the middle age group and up. I guess even for the young people as well. I have been really thinking about what this world, our country, my life, and my family's life could look like in ten years. I have heard some comments about us actually being in the literal last days, which I thought kind of humorous because I have thought that the 2020s, specifically near the end, would be the actual last days. I've thought about that for fifteen to twenty years now. I know a lot of people have studied it much more than me. But logically, if Jesus was going to fulfill the second half of His seven-year ministry on the earth and He fulfilled the first three and a half years when he came and died on the cross, it would seem to me that the actual 2,000 years later that He would come would be, well, 2000 years later which would put us sometime in the twenties. And quite frankly, the way the world is going, I could very easily see that. But you will have to decide in your own heart if you believe that is the case or not.

Let's say I am completely way off, and the Lord doesn't come back for another 200 years. Not going to happen but let's just say that's the case. I am in my middle forties. At best, in forty years, all my dreams (whether fulfilled or not), my accomplishments, failures, loss of loved ones, popularity (which is not trending up from what I can see, and that's okay), all the bucks I've killed... or missed, everything will not matter one bit.

Do you realize how short this life really is? I look at my life, and there are definitely some things I wanted to do, some bucket list stuff, specifically as a hunter, that I am thinking probably never will happen. I dream about a decent size house (a couple of thousand square feet) on, oh, I don't know, 150 acres of prime hunting land, but you know what, it literally doesn't matter whether it happens or not. Forty years tops for me, and it won't mean a single thing. Think of how hard we strive for certain things, and in many cases nothing is wrong with that. But Solomon had it right, surprise when he said all is vanity. Because all the things that mean so much to us now will mean nothing when we breathe our last or the Lord returns. To me, that helps me just breathe easy, just realizing that these things aren't really that important, and my dreams fulfilled or not, are not the true measure of the person I am.

We often mention that eternity will be so nice because there will be no more pain and sorrow. That certainly is true and a wonderful reason to look forward to eternity. But how about this food for thought, the things you wanted to accomplish in life, the dreams you had that maybe you will never get to see, when you get to heaven, those dreams you never saw come to pass will pale in comparison to what you will have when you enter eternity. It won't matter to you at all that you didn't get to achieve those things. Does it really matter if I get my 160-acre hunting land with my nice house here? It will be a laughable thought compared to what I have on the other side of eternity.

I know it's time for me to get my eyes more and more off this silly temporal stuff. There's nothing wrong with pursuing it within balance, just no reason to set my heart on it because it's meaningless in the big scheme of things. It's time to get our eyes on heaven and what that will be like and stop moaning and complaining about what we don't have here or what we might not ever have.

I don't know how heaven will all work except it will be better than my wildest dreams. But I could see the Lord saying to me, "Remember that 160-acre farm you wanted with the nice house in the country? Here, here is a 160,000-acre farm that is yours." My next question would be, "Is there Whitetails on it?" Just kidding... I think. My point in all this is, heaven is going to be so much better than anything we could have possibly achieved here on this earth. I am willing to forgo some dreams and aspirations, some earthly benefits and enjoyments, if the Lord chooses not to give them, knowing that in just a few short years for me, it will literally mean nothing. Then a whole new world of possibilities will open up to me that I will get to do and achieve.

And maybe, possibly, hopefully, the Lord does come back sooner rather than later. And we get to enter into that whole new world of pure marvel where the disappointments and cares of this world will dissipate as we step off our lifeboat onto the beaches of heaven's shore!

It'll be worth it!

WILL NOT THE JUDGE OF ALL THE EARTH DO RIGHTLY

Here is an interesting thought that caught my attention several years back now. It has really helped me when I have prayed over the years, and it feels like nothing is happening. To be honest, the three answers that people use to say how God answers our prayer may be true, but it feels more like a pat answer than really understanding what may be happening with what appears to be unanswered prayer. "Yes," "no," and "not right now." Again, I am not saying they are not accurate to how God responds. It's just, to me, it doesn't really scratch the itch of wanting to know what is going on.

The well-known story in the Bible that has really helped me is the Story of Abraham interceding for his nephew Lot when God was going to destroy Sodom and Gomorrah. Yeah, I know God of the Old Testament. He doesn't do that stuff anymore. Joking, of course! But there is a part of that story that I think is often overlooked, and yet it really has helped me. I am going to go purely from my remembrance of the story, but you can check it out and see that I am accurate in my explanation.

God visits Abraham, and in the process of fellowshipping with Abraham, God tells Abraham he is going to destroy Sodom and Gomorrah because of how evil they are. The two angels that were with God, head to Sodom and Gomorrah, and Abraham is left alone with God. And so begins one of the best examples of interceding with God for the cities (or was it) in the entire Bible, if you ask me. Abraham starts by asking God if he is going to destroy the righteous with the wicked and says suppose there are fifty righteous people there. Will you save the city? As he begins to intercede, he says in Genesis 18:25, "Will not the Judge of all the earth do what is right" And over some intense interceding,

Abraham talks God down to saving the cities for ten righteous people. After Abraham gets God down to ten people, Abraham clearly is satisfied, thinking there *had* to be ten righteous people in those cities, and so he stopped, and they go their separate ways, and Abraham is out of the picture now. The problem was, there weren't ten righteous people.

Then, as Paul Harvey said, "And now for the rest of the story." The angels go down to the city and get Lot, his wife, and two daughters out, and they destroy the city.

Here is the part that really helped me. After Abraham and God separate, It tells the complete story of what happened, pretty dramatic actually, and the next time Abraham comes back into the story, it says he arose and looked over the valley and saw that Sodom and Gomorrah lay in ruins.

Think about this, Abraham prayed that God would save the cities for ten righteous people's sake, and the next time he comes into the picture, he is overlooking a valley that lay burnt in ruins.

If you are Abraham, standing there looking over the valley, did God answer your prayer? Well, of course, He did. But Abraham didn't know that. The angels saved Lot and his daughters by dragging them out of the city. I think that in Abraham's interceding, that was primarily who he was trying to save. But his prayer wasn't quite worded exactly how he was hoping it would. The beautiful thing was that God knew Abraham's heart and still was able to answer Abraham's true intentions for interceding better than Abraham even was asking while doing what He set out to do in His sovereignty.

But *here* is the most amazing part of the story to me and what really helped me in my prayer life for those times when it "appears" nothing is happening. Remember what I said happened when Abraham was brought back onto the scene? It says he looked over a city that lay in ruins. By *all* accounts, Abraham had no idea that his nephew Lot and company had been saved. We so easily forget in our social media, over-communicated society that Abraham didn't have a phone, He didn't have an email address, and there wasn't even the pony express back then. Abraham had zero clue that Lot had been saved. He put it all on the line, interceding with God, walks out the next day, and the cities are gone, destroyed. How did Abraham know Lot was saved? There is no account of them ever connecting again. There is no account that Abraham knew that Lot made it. He certainly didn't know at that moment he saw the city in ashes. By all accounts, Abraham's prayers were not answered based on what he saw with his eyes. But remember what Abraham was resting in, "Will not the judge of the earth do right"? Abraham trusted in His God no matter what appeared to be the case, and he understood that whatever actually did happen, God was just in his decision.

Just because you have prayed perhaps for years and it appears your prayers are not answered doesn't mean that they aren't and doesn't mean that they aren't answered in the way you want. It could be better, and only eternity will make clear what you had no awareness of. We have *no idea* how the Lord works in our prayers, as He has a *much* bigger picture than we do. God answered Abraham's prayer when it absolutely looked the exact opposite. It is very likely Abraham never knew righteous Lot's life was saved until he saw Him again in paradise. The whole time thinking Lot was dead. It is *very* possible that your prayer that you have been praying and has not been answered actually *has* been answered or will be answered in a much better way than you could have ever known to pray.

The prayer of a righteous person avails much. Doesn't mean we will always see the answer, but your prayer and my prayer are doing something. That's where faith comes in. We pray the best we can, like Abraham, and then we trust the sovereignty of God to answer it how He sees fit. I firmly believe that every single Christian that stands before God, when we stand before God, is going to be blown away by the answers to prayers they thought were never answered or appeared even to be a resounding "no" to our prayer.

I can tell you I have a few of them for sure that I really want to see what was happening when I was praying! Believing prayer is never a waste of time. It's never fruitless!

So, keep at it, continue to pray, and pray hard. And regardless of what your natural eyes may see, even if it looks like He didn't listen, or it appears His answer was "no," remember this rhetorical question, "Will not the Judge of all the earth do right?"

DO NOT BECOME WEARY

I can't tell you how hard it was to get up at 4:50 in the morning, get ready and drive an hour to my spot to go deer hunting. I worked right up until about 10:30 p.m. and then went inside, got my stuff ready, showered, and got to bed well past eleven. It's been a long season, some ups, some downs, and part of me, a large part, is content with what has happened and willing to sleep in that extra little bit each morning and forgo the morning hunts. But I still have a buck tag unfilled, and that is what is gnawing at the other part of me. I want to fill this tag! Certainly a mixed bag of feelings. I don't do well historically in the late season as in… I've never killed a buck in the late season. I want to get that monkey off my back. The question is, how badly do I want it? It appears the way in life is for "most" people. To succeed in any area of life, you are going to have to work at it and hard. For most of us, nothing comes easy. The hard part can be when we work so hard for so long, and there don't appear to be any results! The temptation is to give up, quit, throw in the towel and forget all the effort that has been put into whatever it is we are trying to achieve.

I am hunting this morning with my very good friend Matt. Knowing I was going to meet him this morning definitely helped me roll out of bed. Someone was going to be waiting for me. That's a whole Devotional in itself. The companionship of friends will help us in life as much as anything. But ultimately, we have to make the choice to continue on, to work for that dream, to work towards a lofty goal, or perhaps to continue fighting to get victory over a particular weakness in your life or my life. Oftentimes those are the hardest and the most discouraging when it comes to working towards overcoming failure. Sometimes that can seem so far away and even impossible. But I am reminded of the simple verse in the Bible—Galatians 6:9. Let us not become weary in doing good, for at the proper time, we will reap a harvest if we do not give up. I have known people who have given up literally right on the cusp of reaching their goals. I have often wondered about things I had given up on if I would have just kept at it a little longer. Today's devotional is just a simple reminder that our hard work and fighting are not in vain... At the "proper time," we *will* reap *if* we do not give up!

Keep at it, my friend! What you are working so hard to achieve or conquer may be just around the corner!

BE THE LIGHT

Today on this very cloudy day, I was driving down the highway... faster than I should have, I'm sure. Naturally wanting to hunt this first night of Michigan muzzleloader season and hopefully beat the crowd (barely did), my mind was racing between work issues and plans for the hunt... and what I was going to eat for lunch! Two banana muffins for breakfast don't cut it for a guy pushing 3,200 ounces, that is! Wow, that's discouraging. At any rate, as I was cresting this hill on the highway, I looked up and saw all these sunlight beams shooting down through the clouds and clear as could be hitting spots on the earth in various different places. All around, there were clouds, but in this one section, there were lots of rays of sunlight beaming through the gray, dreary sky! Immediately the thought came to me of the verse in the Bible that says in Matthew 5:16, "Let your light so shine before men, that they may see your good works, and glorify your Father which is in heaven."

We are living in very dark days. Oh, not just because of a botched political atmosphere... but rather because gross darkness is covering the entire earth. Just like those clouds dark and gray, the earth is covered in sin and those who scheme sinful acts. Sure there have been times like that in the past, but because of lack of communication, there were blotches around the world. Now due to the attempted globalization of the world, it's covering the whole earth. But somehow, some way, we are called to be just like those light beams that burst forth through the mist and fog and shine the light of Jesus to a world covered in darkness. No sense listing all the ways that we could do that... we can all read the Bible, which is filled with great examples and suggestions... What I would suggest, though, as I am doing myself, is to examine myself and see if my light is one of those lights that is bursting through the clouds and reflecting the sun, or is my light so weak that it doesn't pierce the first layer! The clouds in this world are thick... which means our lights need to be as bright as they have ever been.

I'll finish with this thought. As soon as I saw those rays of light, my immediate reaction was to look up and follow the ray of light through the clouds... the second half of that verse says, "That they may see your good works, and glorify your Father which is in heaven." When we interact with the world, is our ray of light causing people to look up to the source of that light, the Light of The World? Or have the clouds drowned out your ray?

LEARNING GOD'S VOICE

I am hunting with my daughter this morning, and it's a beautiful morning as the sun is creeping up through the trees. It's cold, not windy, and mostly sunny! The kind of mornings you hope for as a hunter... just no deer... yet! One thing there is plenty of is squirrels. I think the property I hunt is the squirrel capital of the world! And the moment the sky starts to go from black to just a slight blue, the squirrel's internal alarm clock goes off, and suddenly, it's like New York City on a Monday morning! I have no problem with squirrels. They are funny and cute... and can, at times, keep you somewhat occupied while you sit and sit... And sit, waiting for a deer to show up. The problem with squirrels is they are loud, and when they get running in those leaves, it might as well be a 250-pound buck walking through the woods. There is not a single hunter alive that hasn't at one time mistaken a squirrel for a deer. The interesting part of what experience does to the hunter is that after a while, he can quickly discount the noise without even seeing the object of the noise because he has learned the cadence of a squirrel in the leaves versus a deer. The last buck I was blessed to harvest, I was actually talking to the video camera doing my morning interview, and there were squirrels everywhere. But as I was talking, I heard something behind me and knew immediately that it was not a squirrel. You can hear it on the video I have of the hunt! The sound was distinctly different. And when I recognized that sound, I immediately turned to see what I ended up shooting. It wasn't that the noise was any louder than the squirrels. It was that the cadence of his steps was different.

That analogy is so accurate to all the voices in the world and in our heads. But there is also another voice, and that is the voice of the Lord! The difficult part can be discerning between the voice of God and other voices, but those who have that relationship with God will tell you that His voice is distinctly different than our own imaginations or the sound of the world. The problem comes in when we either aren't listening or we don't have the relationship with God to decipher between the different voices. I think for every Christian, there is always a learning process or a refining process. There can be so many reasons why we may jump the gun on a voice we think is God's when it's not. What I am learning and seeing in my own life and the lives of others is that with time and experience, we end up running down fewer rabbit trails thinking it's God than we did at the beginning of our journey, or as my earlier analogy goes, our heart rate doesn't jump to eighty beats a second every time we hear a squirrel move. We hear the sound and quickly realize it's not the right sound.

Here are just a couple of things I have learned and am learning about hearing the voice of God that hopefully will be helpful to you.

1. First, it's different. As I said, God doesn't speak the same way the world speaks. It's rarely, if ever, audible, but at times can be so clear it might as well be audible. When He speaks, it's usually completely unexpected and out of the blue. The time is completely unnatural to what you would think in your mind, and in most cases, you would never conjure up the thought on your own. If those two things happen, there is a good chance the Lord may be speaking and not last night's pizza.

2. God is not a chatter bug. One thing he never does is use run-on sentences. His words, or however He chooses to speak, is very much to the point. I mentioned "however" God chooses to speak. Oftentimes God doesn't even use words. So many times in my life, perhaps more than any other way, He used circumstances, and when it happened, I immediately knew God was speaking and what he was saying. As I said before, his voice is distinct and very unique. He is not confined to our method of communicating.

3. Perhaps one of the best tests for discerning the voice of the Lord is the "Mary Test." Time and again, the Gospels say, "Mary hid these things in her heart." What I am learning is that oftentimes when we think God speaks, our best immediate action is to hide it in our hearts and sit on it.

God never seems to be in a hurry, and neither should we. In most cases, especially large decisions, there is almost always confirmation. God usually speaks more than once. And that keeps us from having to jump the gun on things where we are not quite sure of what voice is talking. God knows our frailty and that we are so limited. Like I said, He isn't a chatter bug, but He doesn't mind confirming His words.

To give one example of what I am referring to with these three points, I will tell you a story that happened to me. It's very sad and yet redemptive as well. One of the happy ending stories.

Many years ago, I had no relationship with several members of my family, including my father. The details of what and why are not important except to say that I am sure much of that reason was due to my own immaturity. Thankfully, over the years of growth, things have changed, which has been a wonderful blessing in my life. That is part of the redemptive story.

One night in my devotions sometime in March or April of that year, I was praying for, quite frankly, everything I could think of. In the process of praying, I began to pray for restoration for my family. Suddenly, I was praying with emotions that I had not experienced in regards to praying for this specific request, as they washed over me, and praying became so easy. I didn't have to even think. The words just flowed out of my mouth as tears flowed from my eyes. As I prayed, I kept using the words restoration and restore. Those two words were stuck in my head, and nearly every sentence I prayed had one of those two words in it. I prayed about it for some time until the emotional urge dissipated, and so I finished my prayer time.

I got up from my uncomfortable kneeling position and walked over to my chair, and grabbed my Bible. I sat down and opened my Bible, and the first page I landed on, the first thing my eye landed on was the phrase, "The Restoration of Israel." Now I ask you, what are the chances that I fervently prayed so desperately for the restoration of family members and I open my Bible to any page out of 1,300 or so pages and the first phrase

I read is "The Restoration of Israel"? Remember number one was that He speaks differently? That was different, and I had just finished praying. I opened His story, and, being sensitive to the spiritual realm through prayer, I *knew* He had just spoken to me. He spoke, and I immediately believed that there was going to be a restoration in my family. I didn't know who or how, or when, but I knew that it was going to happen.

Number two was that God is not a chatter bug. I didn't get into this big conversation with Him. Quite frankly, I never have. It was one phrase from the Bible that was the exact language I was using in my prayer. I could not have conjured up that crazy idea of going from prayer to opening to the exact page with that phrase right at the top. It was simple, to the point, and yet extremely clear. So much so that I told a few of my closest friends that the Lord had spoken to me that there was going to be a restoration.

Number three was "The Mary Test," hiding what the Lord spoke in my heart. Like I said, I had told a few people close to me, but I certainly never shouted it from the house top. I tucked it down in my heart and continued living. I didn't start sending hints to family members through other relationship avenues. I just let God do whatever He was going to do.

Jump all the way to October of that year. It was a Sunday morning, and I was up at the front of the church, where I played my instrument along with others for our worship service. I minded my own business before the service started and was preparing my mind to worship the Lord when a friend walked up to me and sat next to me, and said, "Do you see who is sitting in the back?" I looked up, and there in the back pew was my father, who I had not seen in ten years. Let's just say I had a wonderful worship service, and right after, I went back to the back of the church where I met my father, and like Jacob and Joseph, I fell on my father's neck and wept. No kissing the neck, though. There are certain lines I won't cross for anyone! Immediately I remembered all the way back in March or April when I was given a word from the Lord, and nearly seven months He brought it to pass. Through that new beginning, it brought sweet, wonderful restoration to other members of the family as well.

One of my favorite sections of scripture is where God was speaking through an evil man named Balaam. Numbers 23:19 says, "God is not a man, that he should lie; neither the son of man, that he should repent: hath he said, and shall he not do it? or hath he spoken, and shall he not make it good?" When God speaks, it's as good as done. And that day, when God spoke to me, I had complete confidence in His Word because I knew if He said it, it *had* to happen.

That is just one of many stories where I could tell you where the Lord has spoken things to me, and I would love to tell more if there was more time. But my primary hope is that maybe you found a couple of tips that help listen for the voice of the Lord. He is talking, and He wants us to hear His voice. Sure, it's very different from how we would talk to people, and it's certainly not as frequent. But the world is trying to drown His voice out, and if we are not careful, we will run after other voices only to find out that at the end of the road, it wasn't what we were expecting, or worse yet... disaster is waiting for us at the end of the road.

MAINTAIN PROPER BOUNDARIES

Towing the Line—what is in us that loves to flirt with danger? I'm not talking about me. I'm talking about you. I'm a pretty safe guy! I don't consider hanging from a tether twenty-three to twenty-five feet wrapped around a tree up in the air very dangerous. It seems quite safe to me. What's worse yet, why do we often love to flirt with sin? Now I can and will include myself. If there is anyone who can identify with the words to that great hymn, "Come Thou Fount Of Every Blessing," it's me, especially that one verse that says, "Prone to wander Lord I feel it, Prone to leave the God I love." If you're honest with yourself, that is you as well. There is something inside us all that loves to push the limits of what is acceptable. Our fallen nature's insatiable desire for worldly pleasure often finds us going places and doing things we would never accept on its own merit or in discussions of morality. The Bible says we are to Abstain from… every appearance… of evil, just the very "appearance" of evil.

I have always looked at that scripture in 1 Thessalonians 5:11 as we need to be setting good examples of our conduct both in church and to the world. And certainly, I think that can apply. But I would also submit to you that there is another meaning as well. Is it possible that when we push the limits to accept what "appears" to be evil, we will eventually cross into the territory of what *is* evil? You see, from my perspective and experience, when we start pushing the boundaries in our life, we are flirting with danger. Sure, we may not cross the line with each flirting with the appearance of evil, but we are building a bad habit of pushing the boundaries of what is acceptable, and we can only push those boundaries so far for so long until, eventually, we step over those lines from "appearance" to what is actually evil conduct in one area of our life or another, usually with our besetting sins. No man who struggles with pornography ever just starts looking without first thinking about it. He entertains and flirts with the idea in his mind without immediately taking every thought captive to the obedience of Christ. He thinks he can get away with it, but eventually, and usually not that far into it, he gives in to the thought and looks with his eyes. Of course, lusting in the mind is already evil, but it's the same way with flirting with the appearance of evil.

Why is it that when a toddler is just a few feet away from a swimming pool, everyone jumps to high alert and goes running over as fast as possible to grab that toddler? It has not fallen in the water. That little bundle of mischief isn't drowning. In fact, it's on as safe and hard ground as it would be if it was a hundred feet away. We do it because they are pushing a boundary that just a few feet the wrong way could cost them their life.

This past summer, a son (also a pastor) of the pastor that we are closely associated with through school was at home, if I understood correctly, studying. The wife went to do some errands and left their one-year-old child with the husband. While the husband was in his study, the baby was able to get out the door of the house, made his way down to the neighbor's pond, and drowned himself. That baby crossed a boundary it was not supposed to cross, and it cost it his life. Certainly a boundary, of course, you would not expect the baby to know to stay within. But we have boundaries that we are very aware of, and yet so often, we want to live so close to that edge.

Abstain from the very "appearance" of evil. That pretty much covers it. Of course, so often, we think we can go to the edge and look over the precipice of morality and think we won't slip. Well, the Bible covers that as well, 1 Corinthians 10:12, "He that thinks he stands, take heed lest he fall." If we think we can push the boundaries and enjoy living in the appearance of evil and not eventually fall into sin, we are deceiving ourselves. Many great men have done so only to ruin their ministries. Certainly, it could be in the area of pornography or sex. Maybe it's financial favors or unhealthy relationships. Maybe it's enjoying that R-rated movie or just two glasses of alcohol at the family party. As I mentioned earlier, pornography never typically starts with just an immediate stumble. Typically, the temptation arises, then there is the flirting with perhaps the movie that we know there is a nude scene in it, but we are going to "skip it," or pictures with lewd or flirtatious women, and eventually we trip into the pool of sin and start to immediately sink. With other sins as well, it's the pressing of the boundaries, the constant erosion of that boundary where eventually there is nothing left to stop us.

The apostle Paul clearly was not of the mindset that we can push it. Fairly often, one or both of my daughters may tell me in regards to a boundary I put in place, "Dad, there is nothing wrong with that," and they, at times, may be right. Often I have to tell them, sure, but what comes next after that erosion of the boundary? Children often don't know what they don't know any more than a one-year-old has no idea that it would drown in a pond. From music to relationships with boys or girls, are they flirting with the appearance of evil, or is there a solid boundary that they can "make no provision for the flesh to fulfill the lust thereof," as Romans 13:14 puts it?

As believers in Jesus, we are not called to walk a "fine line" but a "narrow road" that keeps us *far* away from the sin of the world by avoiding even the very appearance of evil! That's a hard line to draw in the sand of hearts that are prone to leave the God we love! But it's a safe boundary that keeps us far from sin and close to God. My prayer is the last part of that verse of the hymn. "Here's my heart, Lord, take and seal it, seal it for thy courts above." Safe and protected, not only from the influence of the world but safe from myself and my own carnal desires!

HOLD FAST TO TRUTH

Truth is irrelevant. It has occurred to me that perhaps in some way, we are missing the bigger picture of what is happening in our country and, quite frankly, the world when it comes to truth. As I have kept somewhat up in current events, it has driven me nuts to see blatant lies that have spilled out of the media over the last several years. Completely fabricating stories as if they were absolute truth. And anyone who would dare reject the lies is attacked and considered a fool. But in this, I believe something much worse is happening than even the media lying about this person or that event. What has happened in our country is that there has been such an erosion of the truth that many people write off everything as either lies, or at least they are so confused that they don't know what the truth is. With each lie that is given credence, it is eroding the very foundation of truth. Second Thessalonians speaks of being in the last days, which it would appear we are,

> Even him, whose coming is after the working of Satan with all power and signs and lying wonders, And with all deceivableness of unrighteousness in them that perish; because they received not the love of the truth, that they might be saved. And for this cause God shall send them strong delusion, that they should believe a lie. That they all might be damned who believed not the truth, but had pleasure in unrighteousness.

The world despises the truth, and as a result, God has given them over to their own desires and caused them to believe a lie. I think we could probably agree that we see that in quite amazing ways now. But as a result, many don't even believe *ANYTHING* because lies have eroded the truth so much. It could be true, but they don't believe it. It could be a lie, and so they don't believe it. There has been so much lying that it has effectively caused people not to believe anything, even though the truth may be smacking them in the face. But that should not be so with Christians. Truth and lies should not be so difficult to discern. We not only have a Book that is filled with Truth, but we should have a relationship with the One who is Truth. If we have those two things, then wading through all the lies shouldn't be too hard. Unfortunately, many of us spend more time though on the news channel than we do on the Bible channel. We spend more time watching than we do reading. Truth is the quintessential foundation of life, and it doesn't change with time or culture. When you apply the truth of the Bible to each situation we face, it really isn't that difficult. As Christians, we can't allow society to blur the line between truth and lies. We must hold fast to truth at any cost because once truth is gone, there is nothing left to stand on, and once objective truth becomes subjective truth, everything becomes opinion, and opinions bring bondage because it's only the *truth* that sets us free!

GOD'S AFTER THE HEART

The idea of perfection in life is a wonderful idea... but also not realistic in many ways. Our lives, as long as we live, will be a continual journey of failure, fighting, and growing, we conquer or get control of something like covetousness, and suddenly we realize we may have an anger issue or some other issue. We get control of that, and then we see our tongue is out of control. Life is an endless journey of refinement. One purification after another of the same issue or some other weakness, which is why King David prayed, "I will not be satisfied until I awake in thy likeness! So what is the key to chronic failure? The heart... It's the heart! How could God approve of David so much with all his blatant failures? Because David was a man after God's own heart. David wanted God's presence. He loved God's ways and fought his entire life to attain as much as he could, knowing that there would not be complete satisfaction in his soul until he awoke in the likeness of Christ. God didn't ignore David's failures. No, there were consequences. But God's final judgment wasn't based on David's works but rather on David's heart. As God said to Samuel (Samuel 16:7b), "For the LORD does not see as man sees; for man looks at the outward appearance, but the LORD looks at the heart." That was how God judged David's life, and that is how He will judge your life and my life. Where's my heart? Where's your heart? Sometimes that judgmental, critical person judging the outward appearance is the one that looks in the mirror, forgetting what manner of person they are on the inside. Sometimes that judgmental person is you looking in the mirror, concentrating on your open failures but forgetting the desire of your heart to do what is right. We make judgments of who we are based on our failures. We often forget the victories, though. God doesn't see you as you see you! He's looking past the mask. He's looking past your failures. And He is looking past your perceived success. He's looking at your heart. So in all your striving, in all your giving this thing and that thing to God, hoping to somehow have our good actions outweigh our bad actions. Start by giving him your heart. Surrender your heart to Him. Make his ways the desire of your heart. Because out of your heart flows the issues of life. Certainly, oftentimes, what we see with our natural eyes is the reflection of our hearts. Certainly, we need to strive for a perfect heart towards Christ and not one that is divided. But if we make and act on intentional decisions to make sure our hearts are right with God, when it's all over, and we stand before Him in all of our outward imperfection, we will have nothing to fear because the thing He wanted most, He had... our heart!

TRUST GOD'S LEADING

Psalm 37:23 and 24:23, "The steps of a good man are ordered by the Lord: and he delighteth in his way. Though he fall, he shall not be utterly cast down: for the Lord upholdeth him with his hand."

Proverbs 3:5 is very similar: "Trust in the Lord with all thine heart; and lean not unto thine own understanding. In all thy ways acknowledge him, and he shall direct thy paths."

What I like about Psalms is that he makes it clear this isn't dependent upon perfection... The Lord is able to still direct our steps, mistakes and all. Because of that, we can have peace realizing that God is able to overcome our failures and complete what he started in us.

Weary Christian, are you tired and confused, feeling like you are just wandering. Rest in God. There is more purpose to each step than you realize, and each misunderstood step is actually leading you somewhere very specific that God only knows... but they are not wasted steps.

FIND YOUR WAY

For all of my childhood, I lived in the country, from about two years old to nineteen years of age. Born in Algonac, Michigan, we moved to Pennsylvania when I was two. Mountains all around us, and a creek right next to one of the two houses we lived in Pennsylvania. We lived there until I was five, and then my father took a pastoral position in a little town called Depauville in New York. Technically we lived in a small town, but it was only 375 people, and living on the edge of the town, the country immediately started about two houses up the street. If that wasn't country enough, when I was nine years old, my parents built a house three miles outside of that little town, and I could walk outside the back door of that house, and if I walked a straight line, it was three miles to the next road which was a dirt road and then a couple more miles after the dirt road till you hit another road. Those may not be exact distances, but close. We did live exactly three miles to the west of the town we moved out of, and then exactly another three miles to the east; there was a larger town, but that couldn't have had more than 1,000 to 1,500 people in it. If you walked directly across the street from our house, you almost immediately started walking down into a valley that was a minimum of 100 feet down, and at the bottom, there was a river that ran all the way out to Lake Ontario. I canoed it a couple of times with my friends because that's what boys do. The stories I could tell of fishing that river, and maybe I will someday, were some of the fondest memories I had as a kid.

As I mentioned, out behind our house was a very large piece of wilderness that would have made any hunter drool at the possibility of hunting it. The problem was, it was owned by the state, and at the time we lived there, it was not huntable because supposedly there was some rare plant that was nowhere else in the country, and as a result, they didn't want it getting destroyed by hunters... you know... because human feet destroy things, but deer, raccoons, coyotes, skunks, woodchucks, porcupines, possums, and every other animal out there apparently knew they were not supposed to step on it. That law did change eventually, and property owners adjoining that piece of property could legally hunt on it. But by then, I was long gone.

This property was a country boy's dream because even though we couldn't hunt it, we could walk it. In fact, the main trail leading onto this state-owned property was literally right at the corner of our property. Once you got about a one-fourth mile back through the woods, the trail ended, but you were well on your way to exploring the wilderness behind our house... and I took advantage.

Me and my next oldest brother of two years would go on many walks back there, sometimes together and sometimes alone. I wasn't more than ten or eleven when I would venture out there myself and roam the woods, weaponless, of course, which was its own torture. But the sheer volume of the property and incredible beauty of this land was still worth the effort even if I couldn't hunt giant swamp bucks and other unknown dinosaur-like animals living back there that no one had ever seen, simply because those animals only lived in my imagination, at least the dinosaur-like ones.

Speaking of dinosaurs. In some of my brother and my Lewis and Clark explorations, we found these enormous flat rocks that were the size of football fields, or at least they felt like it, and there were... wait for it... fish fossils all over these rocks. True story. We actually convinced our science teacher to take a field trip out there, and all the students in high school ninth grade and up... so that was like ten total, walked way out into these woods to see these fossils. My brother and I felt pretty important leading such an expedition. Remember when I said earlier, there was a river a good hundred feet below where our house sat? Makes you wonder when all the fossils happened! My guess was roughly about... 142 billion... seconds ago. Roughly the time of Noah's flood.

These rocks were not hard to find because we had been back in those woods so much we knew it like the back of our hand, whatever that means. I didn't grow up in the country learning directions by road names or towns. For me, it was this tree, that stump, that boulder, and that creek. I had the woods all mapped out based on landmarks, and I never worried about getting lost because I was so familiar with them. I walked all over, and once I saw one of my landmarks, I knew which way it was pointing me home... that is, until this one time.

I was around twelve, my next oldest brother Steve was fourteen, and my oldest brother Dan was eighteen. As I mentioned, Steve and I had been back there a bunch over the years. But I had never gone back there with Dan. He wasn't quite into the whole exploring thing quite like Steve and I were, but for some reason, this evening, he decided to go out for a hike with me. Steve, in fact, was out bow hunting that night on another piece of property with my father and another man from the church. He actually missed a buck that evening which plays into the story later on.

As Dan and I got back into the woods, we started roaming around as I had always done. We saw the fossils, and then we walked in other areas enjoying the scenery as it was incredibly diverse back there. We soon realized it was getting dark, and we needed to head back home. The problem was, I could no longer recognize my landmarks in the low light, and to be quite honest, because Dan was so much older, I let him lead even though he had not the experience I had back in those woods. As a result, we roamed around for quite a while, not knowing where we were. We were lost. We weren't worried we were going to die or anything, but still being lost in the woods in the dark... With dinosaur-like animals hiding out there somewhere was kind of spooky. We had no choice but to keep walking. Now it was pretty much pitch black aside from the starlit night, and our pupils being the size of gumballs, we trudged on, trying to make sure we didn't walk in circles so we would eventually end up hitting a road or some house along a road. Essentially, a perfect setting to start a horror movie. Two brothers, lost in the woods, happen upon an old abandoned cabin, and yet we see a single candle lit through a broken window with a cat moaning from somewhere inside. As we approach, a night owl hoots in the pine tree above us, alerting the mad scientist of our arrival, and a coyote howls off in the distance on a full moon night. Now you know how I could imagine dinosaur-like creatures out there tracking us down.

Long story short, as we kept walking, we started to hear a car horn go off and realized we were headed for a road. That horn gave us direction, and as we got closer, we realized it was our mom driving up and down the road looking for us. Steve had shot at a buck and thought he hit it, and we needed to go help him track it. Except he didn't hit it. So there's that. But thankfully, his call to my mom to see if we could come and track was what caused her to come looking for us, and ultimately her horn was what led us to the road. Incidentally, we ended up on our road, but nearly a mile east of our house. We were truly lost.

Recently, for whatever reason, I was reminded of that experience. I had never truly been lost before that and only lost one other time since, a couple of years back. But other than trying to bog my way through a swamp, GPS made it much easier to find my way out. But that night all those years ago, we were definitely lost.

There are some valuable lessons to learn from that experience, and not just for hiking, but for life. I would say the first and most obvious would be that regardless of how confident you are in what you know, you should always take a compass. A compass is possibly the best piece of equipment you could take on long hikes because if you know how to use it, it will always lead you home. You cannot get lost with a compass. Why? Because it always points due North.

We live in a world that has completely lost its compass, its moral compass. Where for the most part, years ago, morality was fairly clear, at least to the masses. Now the tables are turned, and the masses are completely clueless about what our nation, our world's moral compass, should be. Even back in the days of my grandfather's time, while many or most didn't profess faith in Christ, they still stole their moral ideas from the pages of scripture. But not anymore. The Bible and the Commandments of God have been removed from schools. Prayer to Christ has been thrown out of our public schools, and we wonder after this has been happening for forty or fifty years, why is our society so lost. Because we threw out the one and only compass that always points North, the Bible, and as a result, the Author of the Bible. We have replaced the Bible in our schools and society with psychiatrists, philosophers, and professors, but almost all of them are pointing a very different way than due north. As a result, our society is stumbling around the tall trees and sharp thorns of life trying to find their way... unsuccessfully, I might add.

The Bible says there is a way that seems right to a man, but the end leads to death. We cannot substitute a single way of God's and expect us to still arrive at our desired destination. It cannot and does not work that way. There is only one true North, and that is Jesus Christ, the Living Word, who gave us His written word. And that written word says He is THE WAY, THE TRUTH, AND THE LIFE. No one else has that role or could fulfill those three roles. The next lessons learned will all piggyback and point to Jesus and His word as the *only* compass we must live by if we are not going to get lost in this world and all its political and social strife.

As I mentioned in the story, it had gotten dark on us, and as a result, we had lost our way. And the reason we lost our way was that I could not see the landmarks that I knew so well in the daylight anymore. I had never walked out there before in the dark. I only knew my markers when I could visibly see them.

The first part of Proverbs 23:10 says not to remove the ancient landmarks. If you remember, back when Israel went into the Promised Land and conquered it, there were a few tribes that stayed on the other side of the Jordan instead of crossing it. They had given Moses and Joshua their word they would help the rest of Israel take over their portions in the Promised Land before they returned back to their homes on the other side of the Jordan River.

The fighting men of the Tribes of Rueben and Gad and half of Manasseh had stayed faithful to their promise, and when every other tribe had received their portion, these tribes returned home. When they got to the Jordan river, they built an altar of memorial there, and when the rest of Israel heard of it, they were angry because they thought they had sacrificed to other gods. The other tribes were literally ready to go destroy them and confronted these three tribes on what they had done. Their explanation after they listened to the rebuke from the rest of Israel was quite profound.

The reason they had built that altar was to create a landmark or a memorial for the generations that followed so that anyone who saw that landmark altar would remember that these three tribes were still part of Israel, and as a way of remembrance, their children and grandchildren wouldn't be cast away from the rest of Israel. It was there to point to and bring to remembrance the truth of what the original agreement was between all the tribes of Israel.

Just like that Landmark in Israel's history, I had certain landmarks that I could follow, and they always led me to the right place, back home. As long as they were still there, I was fine. But once I could no longer see them, in this case, they were not moved but invisible. I lost my way.

This truth is the same with us as believers and even true in society. It's amazing to me how society borrows so much from the Bible but is not willing to serve the God of the Bible. Unfortunately, this same problem, in some ways, has crept into the church. Some who read this may not like that statement, but I believe it's the truth.

Because of changing culture and even somewhat pure intentions at times, the church has moved the ancient landmarks in an attempt to appeal to the changing culture. We have created fancy Sunday sermons instead of preaching the clear Word of God. Many pastors have turned to life coaching messages and motivational speeches rather than actual preaching. We have changed our style of "worship" to attract a different crowd. The church, or at least people in the church, have adjusted the standard of modesty over the years to not be quite like the world but not too far behind either. We have even changed how we witness to the world that is condemned. We have concentrated on the Love of God based on pretty much one verse but have ignored the fact that the condemned are abiding under the wrath of God... The same chapter, incidentally. Why? Why has much of the church done this? Because the ancient landmarks didn't seem to get the desired results we were looking for.

I think it's important if you are a believer in Jesus to remember that when God told Israel they were to sacrifice in certain ways. He often said this would be a procedure that they would do *"forever."* So for the next nearly 1,300 years, God was completely content with Israel doing the same sacrifices, the same way, without changing a single thing. We need to remember that when God is pleased with something, He will *always* be pleased with that something. He doesn't change based on getting bored. He is not influenced by changing cultures. We are to get on God's plan. He never will adjust His to ours.

But the landmarks all through Christendom have been changing. And do I need to point to the obvious fallout of that? Mega churches with false teachers getting rich on the backs of their flock. TV shows that beg people for money prey on elderly vulnerable men and women. How about these false healers acting like they are knocking people over by the power of the Holy Spirit and healing them, deceiving so many by thinking miracles are happening when in fact, demons are controlling the service. Other places have super fancy programs and shows where people get all emotional like they are meeting God. They get happy for a couple of hours, but their hearts are not changed. Immorality in our youth is at an all-time high. How about this one, I know I'm going to step on toes here, but I believe it makes my point perfectly clear, women pastors. The Bible is as cut and dry on women pastors as it is *thou shalt not steal*. But that is a very unpopular stance in the 21st century, so *many* leaders have gone to great lengths to reinterpret the black text of scripture by finding hidden "meanings" in the white spaces between the black letters. That truth Paul made very clear has been the ancient landmark by enlarge of the church for 2,000 years. It's only in the last fifty years or so that church leaders have begun to change their opinion. All these things are leading multiplied hundreds of thousands of immature sheep astray, just in America alone.

Why? Because we have moved the ancient landmarks. We have decided that God's ways are outdated and not relevant to the 21st century. And as a result, we have lost our way. Christians justifying homosexuality and abortion, supporting political leaders that openly defy God and any of His principles because they think there was a better financial package with that leader.

There is one and only one way, and that is Jesus Christ, and His Word that He left us is *filled* with ancient landmarks for us to follow. And if we choose not to follow them, we will not have the impact on the world that we say we want, regardless of how many fancy programs and evangelistic tools we have at our disposal. The world needs to be shown one way and how to walk in that one way. We can't expect the world to walk in a way that we are not willing to walk in ourselves.

The last thought that came to mind from my experience so many years ago is this, who are you following? While my brother was quite a bit older than me, he did not have the experience that I had out there, and as a result, I was following someone who didn't know their own way, much less helping me find the right way. Obviously, this had nothing to do with his character but rather just lack of experience.

But apply the same question to the people we are following and getting fed from, and I would ask you, are they leading you down the right path? Or are they leading you astray? Perhaps it may be pure intentions but lack of experience. Or, or... Have they intentionally removed ancient landmarks of scripture to fill their pews and line their pockets or set them on the pedestal of popularity? The Bible says that leaders will be judged more strictly because of the responsibility they carry. Ask Moses about that one. Is the leader you are following straying from the ancient landmarks or are they holding true to the never-changing landmarks found in the Bible?

Maybe you are that leader. What are you doing? Do you let political, and I mean church politics, opinion sway your convictions of what the Bible says? Perhaps, pressure from parishioners is pushing you to move the boundaries. Maybe your group, whether a church or small group, is not growing quite like you want it, so you are feeling the pressure to change your tactics to "draw" more people in, and yet those "tactics" are not in line with scripture. Or, there may be other things you are doing that are not according to the Bible because they are not popular opinions anymore.

I would challenge you to get back to finding what the ancient landmarks are in the word of God so that you and all those that follow you do not get lost in the way. There is so much deception in and outside the church that the people of God need leaders that know God's ways and boldly proclaim, "This is the way. Follow me as I follow Christ." Will you be that leader? Will you stand against the changing tide and be a pillar that the waves of illegitimate change do not move?

There is a way that seems right to a man, but that way leads to death. God has *a way*, and He has given us ancient landmarks all along that way to follow. So that in a world of confusion and changing morality, just like a lighthouse on a stormy, wind-blown, wave-crashing night, we can hold true to our compass and find our way safely, this time, to our heavenly home!

STRENGTHS BECOMING WEAKNESS

My parents were fairly gifted musically, and that gene apparently was passed down to us children to some degree. Based on what I saw, it appears my mom was more gifted than my father but even he was no slouch when it came to music. My dad had a decent ear to hear music, but my mom, looking back, I would say her ear for music was quite exceptional. It's no surprise considering the musical genes in her family. One great uncle was a famous trombone player and quite well known. Years ago, I looked him up online, and in the article I read, he was considered in the top ten best in the world at the time. True or not, just to be recognized by anyone like that, you have to be phenomenal, and he was.

Another one of my uncles on my mother's side played violin, I believe, in the DSO and was also quite accomplished on the trumpet, if I understood correctly. These are uncles I never knew but carried their own reputation based on their abilities. Eight or nine years ago now, maybe longer, my grandma was visiting us here in Michigan, and she told me that this great uncle of mine played jazz in a restaurant in Grosse Pointe. So we loaded up the family and took my grandma to go see him. The place was quite empty, aside from a couple of other people there eating, and I think we ordered a French fries or something like that. Basically, there were about five old people in their eighties setting the buttons of their instruments on fire as they tore up and down and all around the musical scale. I was blown away! It was a memorable experience.

I say all that just as a way of referring to my first statement that musical ability was passed down to us four boys to some degree. We all played instruments and were fairly capable of them. When I was thirteen years old, I was permitted to play my saxophone in our church worship services. I never heard any complaints, so apparently, I did reasonably well.

When I was nine years old, my parents bought me a used Yamaha Saxophone that now I have since passed on to one of my boys, who is learning to play it. It really wasn't my ability to read notes that helped me learn to play. It was my ability to hear the notes that helped me navigate my way through solos and band songs, etc. And I wasn't the only one. Like my mom, all of us boys were pretty proficient at playing by ear, never needing sheet music to play our church worship songs, though I think all three of my brothers were much more proficient than me at reading sheet music.

I've since picked up the trumpet about fourteen years ago and taught myself to play. I never had a lesson, just taught myself. By no means do I consider myself as good on the trumpet as I was on the saxophone, but again, they let me play it in our worship services, so I must be at least reasonable at it. But if you were to ask me how I know which buttons to push, I would tell you I have no idea. I just do... most of the time. I'm not reading notes, and if you put sheet music in front of me, it would ruin me. What really would happen is I would stumble my way through it, and as soon as I got the melody, I would remember it and start playing by ear. That's just how I have always done it.

Like the rest of my family, I have always considered being able to play music by ear to the degree we can to be a tremendous strength. In fact, I knew a lady that had perfect pitch, but she could barely play by ear and yet was an amazing piano player. Go figure. So I had this pretty good strength that was a plus for music. The problem was I also had this terrible weakness in music as well, and that was... playing by ear. Yes, my greatest strength was also my greatest weakness.

You see, my ability to play music by ear was the reason that I never really learned how to play by notes. Oh, if you put a note in front of me right now, I could tell you what note it was but put several notes in front of me at one time, and I would be the musical sloth trying to work my way through a piece until I figured it out by my ear and then memorized it. Where this weakness shows up, in particular, is when I am given sheet music to sing. I essentially have to have someone plink out the notes for me on a piano because trying to read notes plus rhythms all at the same time is quite difficult for me. And really, until I can hear it and memorize it, I am behind everyone else who can read with trying to learn my part. Thankfully lots of practices help me catch up. But it's not fun, and it is quite uncomfortable when around those who are proficient at reading music. All because I allowed strength to create weakness in me.

I would say very often, and perhaps most often, this scenario applies to real-life situations rather than just someone who wants to play music. I could point out all sorts of scenarios, but let's just take a couple. How about someone who is extremely merciful. They are motivated by mercy every chance they have, whether it's something done against them or in a situation where they have leadership and pass judgment and possible consequences on someone, always showing mercy. What a tremendous strength and, quite frankly, a rare strength. I would dare say most people are not quite so merciful, especially when it's an atrocity against them. But is showing mercy always a strength? I would say no. In fact, I would say, at times, it could be extremely damaging to someone. Why? Because some people need to suffer the consequences of their actions, to feel the pain of their poor choices to learn not to do them again. Pain is a powerful teacher.

I think one of the hardest places to find this balance is with raising kids, especially the baby of the family. Boy, oh boy, do I find myself in a tug of war between mercy and discipline with my kids. As a father that would kill, die and do whatever is necessary to protect my children, the immediate response for me is to help remedy the situation even when it's their fault. From my experience, when the kids are young, you have a lot more zeal and really lack of discernment in so many ways, and it's much easier to practice the discipline part of parenting without much thought to cause and effect. But as you get older and have more experience, and quite frankly, start to connect with your kids on a more mature level, it becomes much harder to discern whether to discipline or show mercy. Everything isn't just disobedience anymore, and often, even their bad choices still had a reason behind them which they assumed to be wise at the time. If you're not careful, your strength may become your biggest weakness.

There is a place for both discipline and mercy, and while you may be great at discipline, there is a time for mercy, and that quality could become a travesty in the wrong situation. And likewise, vice versa.

What is my point to all of this? To identify our strengths and also make the connection how our strengths can turn on us if we are not careful with balancing them correctly. Not that we can ever get it right all the time. But we can be right more than wrong if we first recognize what our strengths are and then understand how they could be our weaknesses as well, then learn to manage them properly.

Spouses, friends, coworkers, church leaders, and even our children can help balance us out in these areas... if you or I have a teachable spirit. Part of the hope of marriage is that the two spouses balance each other out, right? One is a spender, which is great for buying Christmas gifts for your kids until you can't pay bills on January 1. One is a saver, which is great until you have plenty of money but won't take the family on a little vacation because you don't want the savings account to drop five hundred dollars when there are thousands of dollars in it.

Here is my hope for you, as I myself, as a father, husband, friend, boss, and someone who is in some capacity of leadership at my church, have to struggle through every day as well, that is, that you will recognize how your greatest strength, may be, in fact, being used against you and perhaps doing more harm than even good in certain situations.

The Bible says that the enemy schemes against us. He's always up to no good, and you have heard the phrase, "If you can't beat 'em, join 'em." That's the slang version. But our adversary is more than willing to do the same, and if he can't destroy your strength, he will most gladly pervert it effectively, making it of no use and, most often, actually damaging to many situations. I have seen actual strengths of people become their greatest weaknesses with life-altering implications for not only themselves but for those around them. All because they didn't recognize the balance of their strength and learn how to manage it properly. No criticism here. I've seen it in my own life. Part of life's regrets is very much centered on something I would consider a strength being completely out of balance and causing much harm as a result.

Like I said, I don't think we will ever get it one hundred percent correct every time. But if we are intentional, we can certainly limit the damage and make sure that the majority of the time, our strengths stay just that, a strength.

PATIENCE TRULY IS A VIRTUE

Hi, I'm Phil, and I'm impatient. There, I said it! Don't get offended if I am honest with you. I do the same with myself. It's all done out of love, of course, seriously. I really am impatient. It's always something I've struggled with, I suppose, and I have even recognized it and worked at fighting it, but the struggle is real. The sad part is, while I know it's a weakness I have to work on, I never really knew the consequences of my impatience until recently while turkey hunting.

I had gotten to my hunting spot. While I was getting ready, the homeowner came out, and we talked for a little bit. He goes back inside the house, and I continue to get ready. While I am videoing myself getting ready for my YouTube channel, suddenly, he comes back out and lets me know there is a big old tom with a couple of hens right in his backyard. He goes back inside, so I hurry up and get ready and make my way to the side of his shed. I peak around the shed, and sure enough, they are out there just pecking away at, hopefully, ticks. The yard is a good size, and the high point is right in the middle of the yard. They are on one side, and I'm on the other. I kneel down behind the shed, get all my camo on, get my other equipment ready and then wait until they disappear behind the high point of the yard. So far, things are going perfectly. They have no idea I'm there.

I peek around the corner of the shed again and watch them until the Tom's big tail fan, which he was using to try and impress the two ladies, disappears over the hump in the ground. I decide I'll sneak around on my side to the back of the property and get down into the woods, set up, and then I'll call to them. Once I get to the back, there is a pine tree that is a perfect spot to tuck in under and blend in, so I get all settled under the pine tree, get my camera set up and get ready to call. I just get settled in, and I look up, and to my utter surprise and delight, the hens are back on top of the knoll and start slowly walking my way. No way the Tom is going to leave the hens alone, and sure enough, he slowly starts to follow with his long thick beard nearly dragging on the ground. The tension is building as one of the hens works off to my left at about fifteen yards. She has no idea I'm there, and I just sit there waiting for the other hen to lead the Tom by me as well. My breathing intensifies, and I have to tell myself to calm down because I'm about ready to hyperventilate from the excitement and adrenaline rush.

Suddenly the hen that the Tom is following decides to go off to my right at about thirty-five yards and down into the creek bottom. Naturally, the big boy decides to follow her and veers off as well to head down to the bottom. There is a giant tree it is going to walk behind, which allows me perfect timing to swivel the camera and get the gun in place. Once it gets past that tree, there is a little opening, and then another smaller tree, where after that smaller tree, there is a rather large opening before it walks off the ledge down to the bottom. I haven't shot very many turkeys, and this seems too good to be true as the Tom works his way off to my right. As he goes behind the tree, I swivel my body and the camera and click off the safety, waiting for him to emerge on the other side. He has no idea I'm there, and all I have to do is wait until he gets past that smaller tree into a large opening, make a couple of yelps to stop him, put the bead on his head, pull the trigger, and just like that it's turkey thighs and burgers for me. That's not what happens. He clears the big tree, my impatience and inexperience kicks in, and as he is moving in that small clearing, I quickly put the bead on his head and pull the trigger. He jumps and is so startled by the shot he doesn't know what to do. So I jumped up, racked another shell in the chamber, ran to where I could see him just over the ledge, and fired off another shot. I missed, and, of course, now he's running, so I pump the action on my gun and fire another, and then another, and then another.

By the time the Tom disappears over the little ridge into the swamp, I am standing there, turkeyless with an empty gun and no shells left on my person. I found it more humorous than anything because it wasn't a giant whitetail buck, but I had still blown a perfect opportunity. The reason I had blown it was because I was impatient. All I had to do was give it some more time, and almost for sure, that turkey would have presented a much better shot. But I couldn't wait. What if I moved and he saw me? What if he turns around behind the tree and goes the other way, and I don't get a shot because I rarely get opportunities like this? What if a hen spooks and scares him? All these things had run through my mind in milliseconds which caused me to rush the shot and, consequently, miss the bird.

But here's the thing, that turkey hunt actually might have been the most successful hunt I've had in years because it opened my eyes to the consequences of my impatience. This is not the first time impatience has cost me dearly when hunting. But this hunt was the first time where I really was able to recognize the problem of why I have had so many unsuccessful hunts in my life. My mind went back to 2009 when I was hunting southern Illinois with a gun. The rut was going crazy, and I was in a prime location. I wanted a big buck, but I hadn't killed very many good bucks by then, so I had an itchy trigger finger. About 1 hour after daylight, a respectable buck came running by me, and I just couldn't wait any longer. I shot it and dropped it forty yards from me. I was so happy with my choice, that was, until a buck that you go to southern IL to hunt came by thirty minutes later at fifty yards, stopped for about twenty seconds as I recorded it on my video camera, and then trotted away having no idea I was there... impatience.

There was the buck I was hunting with my brother in Southern Ohio that walked through my shooting lane twice at twenty yards but never stopped the whole time I had my bow drawn. Finally, with a loud grunt, it stopped, but it was quartering hard toward me. It didn't matter, it had stopped, and I couldn't wait any longer. So, I put the pin on him and quickly released an arrow, only to hit a small tree right in front of him that I didn't see... Impatience. I got a consolation prize about five minutes later on a respectable buck. But the one I had missed was really the kind of buck you go to a Whitetail Outfitter in southern Ohio for.

How about the time two years ago on Michigan public property, I had a very nice buck coming in. He was at thirty-five yards and had no idea I was there, aside from the fact that he heard me grunt and was coming in to kick the rear end of another buck he thought was there. He was angling toward me perfectly and would have walked by me at about fifteen yards, but again I couldn't wait. As he walked past the sapling at thirty-five yards, which is a very doable shot for me, he stopped, and I let the arrow fly. It was headed perfectly, except at thirty-five yards, I didn't see the tiny twig right in front of his vitals, and my arrow hit that twig perfectly and deflected my arrow entirely below the buck. It's all on film for me to weep over for the rest of my life. Buck gone, damage done, except it wasn't. I got upset and decided to get down on one of the best days of buck movement I had ever seen. I was three-fourths of the way down the tree when I heard leaves rustling and making noise. I turned my body to see a smaller but shooter buck with its nose to the ground working its way right by my tree. I hung onto the tree about seven feet off the ground, and that buck walked by me at seven yards and had no idea I was there as it drifted off into the swamp... Impatience.

What happened that day when I missed that turkey was the light bulb finally went on in my head, and I suddenly realized that I had an Achilles' heel when it came to hunting. I was an impatient hunter. Every year I have put myself into a position to get shots at the game I am after, namely whitetail bucks, and almost every time, I blow it for no other reason than I am impatient. I could bore you with another ten to fifteen times, but nearly every single missed opportunity I have had comes down to being impatient and rushing the shot or moving too soon, like last year, on the ground, with an eight-point buck twelve yards away that I just couldn't wait for him to walk through my shooting lane. I had to try and force the shot. He saw me move, and that was all she wrote. Sorry, the most recent one, so I had to get it off my chest.

Now that I have realized this frustrating weakness and have

recognized the consequences of my impatience, what have I learned? Be patient! But that's easier said than done. When you build a bad habit, and it basically becomes instinct, how do you change your typical MO? For one, recognizing what I have lost and embracing the frustration of my actions is one way to avoid going down the same well-worn trail as before. What my antler collection could look like now versus what it is could be drastically different if I had played my cards differently. But I didn't, and there is nothing wrong with reminding myself of that fact, so long as it inspires me to change my habits and not discourage me into giving up... And that's definitely not going to happen.

While there is plenty of room for discussion about why impatience is wrong, I think that possibly the biggest reason to avoid impatience is that it often causes you to miss out on the best that is to come. Very often, there is something better, bigger, and more beneficial to you and me that would come our way if we just didn't allow impatience to cause us to settle for something less than the best.

What I realized when it comes to my hunting is that I have to learn to exercise patience in such a way that I need to be willing to let the deer, or turkey, walk away if it doesn't present the right opportunity. I have to be willing to sometimes lose the opportunity to wait for a better one. For me, that is hard because I don't get a bunch of opportunities with hunting. But in my case, statistics show that I will most likely come away empty-handed anyway. So why not just hold out until the right opportunity presents itself? Certainly, success can help me have some patience knowing I can get it done by waiting for the right time to release that arrow or pull that trigger. But failure can also be and usually is the best teacher. I have plenty of failed lessons under my belt to look back on and realize things could be much different had I learned this lesson much earlier in life. But as they say, better late than never.

What about you? Are you pushing things through when it's just not time? Perhaps you're striving for something that God has decided you're not ready for yet. Are you trying to force doors open that are shut quite securely, but you just don't want to wait? At time's patience is the toughest when the opportunity comes calling, but you know it's not the right opportunity or God's timing. Waiting is a very hard game to play, especially in this fast-food drive-through society, although things are changing, and it's not so "fast food" anymore. I wish learning patience and waiting for bucks to walk by was the only area I needed to learn this beneficial virtue. But I'm trying to learn that there is plenty of time to do the things I'm meant to do, and when God says I'm ready, then it will be time. Impatience is simply ignoring God's time frame and elevating our timing over His. When I'm not in the moment, I can't imagine how ignoring God's timing is ever going to work out in my favor. But in that moment, it's often much more difficult to remember.

For much of my life, patience has been the forgotten virtue that sat in the back corner of the seller, collecting dust. But my recent experience with the fortunate Tom caused me to realize I needed to pull out that dusty goodness from the mental seller, brush it off, and start applying it to every area of my life that requires its services. After all, as the old saying goes, "Good things come to those who wait."

Psalm 27:14: "Wait on the Lord: be of good courage, and he shall strengthen thine heart: wait, I say, on the Lord."

CPSIA information can be obtained
at www.ICGtesting.com
Printed in the USA
LVHW020524180922
728572LV00011B/377

9 798887 380612